DESCRIPTION

BY

MONICA WOOD

WRITER'S DIGEST BOOKS
CINCINNATI, OHIO

For Dan Abbott—teacher, craftsman, friend.

ABOUT THE AUTHOR

Monica Wood is the author of two novels, *My Only Story* and *Secret Language.* She is also the author of several teaching guides to contemporary literature. Her short stories have been widely published, and collected in such anthologies as *Best American Mystery Stories, Twenty Timeless Stories, Fiction's Many Worlds,* and *The Pushcart Prize Anthology.*

Description. Copyright © 1995 by Monica Wood. Printed and bound in the United States of America. All rights reserved. No part of this book may be reproduced in any form or by any electronic or mechanical means including information storage and retrieval systems without permission in writing from the publisher, except by a reviewer, who may quote brief passages in a review. Published by Writer's Digest Books, an imprint of F+W Publications, Inc., 4700 East Galbraith Road, Cincinnati, Ohio 45236. (800) 289-0963. First paperback edition 1999.

Other fine Writer's Digest Books are available from your local bookstore or direct from the publisher.

Visit our Web site at www.writersdigest.com for information on more resources for writers.

To receive a free weekly e-mail newsletter delivering tips and updates about writing and about Writer's Digest products, send an e-mail with the message "Subscribe Newsletter" to newsletter-request@writersdigest.com or register directly at our Web site at www.writersdigest.com.

10 09 08 07 06   11 10 9 8 7

Library of Congress has catalogued hard copy edition as follows:

Wood, Monica
    Description / by Monica Wood.
       p.   cm.—(Elements of fiction writing)
    Includes index.
    ISBN-13: 978-0-89879-681-0 (hardcover)
    ISBN-10: 0-89879-681-4 (hardcover)

    ISBN-13: 978-0-89879-908-8 (pbk. : alk. paper)
    ISBN-10: 0-89879-908-2 (pbk. : alk. paper)
    1. Fiction—Technique.   2. Narration (Rhetoric)   3. Description (Rhetoric)
    I. Title.   II. Series.
PN3383.N35W66   1995
808.3—dc20   95-19578
                                                           CIP

Edited by Jack Heffron
Designed by Angela Lennert Wilcox

CONTENTS

INTRODUCTION

Description is not so much an element of fiction as its very essence; it is the creation of mental images that allow readers to fully experience a story. When you write a story, you offer an account of a chain of events, the characters that inhabit those events, and the places in which those events occur. How you describe those events, characters, and places affects your readers' perceptions.

Every technical decision you make during the writing of a new story—from the length of your sentences to your choice of point of view—becomes part of that story's description. The statement "John showed up with a gun" describes an event. "John arrived, pistol glinting in his hand" describes the same event with a little more pizazz. Your instinct for jazzing up a plain declarative sentence has repercussions, however, because the rewrite describes something beyond a simple action. For starters, the rewrite gives us a bit of atmosphere— "glinting" suggests light and gives the gun an aura of menace. Second, it tells us something about the observer, who uses the more accurate word "pistol," and is aware of the "glinting." Third, it suggests something about John's state of mind: a man with a glinting pistol must surely be aching to pull the trigger, whereas a man who simply shows up with a gun could have any number of intentions. The mental images in the rewrite are profoundly different from those in the original sentence. Even the smallest decisions about description can affect a story in countless subtle ways.

When you write, you create a fictional world. You may describe that world in lyrical prose fashioned around a central metaphor; you may opt for a stark, straightforward telling that uses few adjectives;

1

you may invent a first-person narrator who uses made-up words; you may render a story entirely in dialogue, evoking characters through the cadence of their voices. Good description takes many forms and does not depend solely on adjectives and adverbs for impact. A statement as simple as "the man wept" may be all the description you need for a particular scene. What makes one story more finished—more "real" and alive—than another is not a matter of adjectives per sentence; it is the *accuracy* and *relevance* of whatever description you do use.

Describing a character as "a beautiful girl who made heads turn" is not especially accurate: she could be Chinese or African, six feet tall or four-foot-nine. Focussing on her "coppery hair" or "deeply flecked eyes" creates a more accurate mental image. If the *fact* of her beauty rather than a literal picture is what you want to convey, however, then a line of dialogue may make for the most accurate description: " 'Isn't she pretty?' Al said." Or you might write, in a one-line paragraph:

She was a beautiful girl.

The sentence, like the character, stands alone. The placement of that sentence accurately evokes the image of a character in a class by herself.

In addition to being accurate, description must be relevant to the story at hand. You need not describe the "old, scarred, rickety maple table in the foyer" when a simple "table in the foyer" will do. A string of adjectives like this—words with similar meaning and impact—doesn't create much of a mental image and may even distract the readers from your fictional world. This is irrelevant description, description for its own sake. If the table is important, then describe it in a way that shows its relevance to the story. The same table described as "a sentry burdened by weeks of unopened mail" becomes an object with a purpose in the household. The description also suggests something about the people in the household—why do they let their mail go for weeks unopened? Remember, you are not merely writing; you are writing a story! It is up to you to guide your readers through the story's events and make sure they don't get lost in a thicket of words and images along the way.

TYPES OF DESCRIPTION

The suggestions and guidelines contained in this book are not designed to alter your natural writing style. Description comes in many forms. The oft-maligned minimalists—many of them brilliant chroniclers of modern life—use spare, economical prose that, paradoxically, opens up a story. A few well-placed details (a half-smoked cigarette, a broken heel, a muddy sunset) can express the essence of a character or place. Other writers are more flamboyant, even rambunctious, with their descriptions: syntactical pyrotechnics spark from every page. Each of these extremes brings its own brand of delight to both writer and reader.

In *A Soldier of the Great War,* novelist Mark Helprin tells an epic tale of war in which descriptions of thunderstorms and moonrises take up pages at a time. Women's faces, the war's grisly battles, ice-laden cliffs, fields, houses, paintings—all are rendered in close, precise, lyrical detail time and again, to the consternation of some readers and the delight of others. Why this much detail? Why not simply tell the story? Because, as the happy reader gradually discovers, *A Soldier of the Great War* is not a tale about war but a tale about beauty. The protagonist is a professor of aesthetics and war veteran at the end of his life, and the story's lyrical descriptions are true to his view of the world. Beauty, we discover, is an affliction, a refuge, an absolute truth. In the final scene, the old soldier/professor watches a flock of swallows being taken down by a hunter. No matter how many are felled, more rise up, banking and fluttering in an exquisite sky. Just as the novel's protagonist has fallen and risen time and again, unable *not* to hope, the swallows keep rising because they know how to do nothing else. It is a memorable scene, a harrowing view of beauty, a metaphor for the novel itself:

> Alessandro turned again to the swallows. Though the sun backlighted them into hallucinatory streaks of silver, he neglected to shield his eyes, and he watched them fill the sky. As the hunter approached the base of the cloud, he made no effort to go quietly or to conceal himself.
>
> Alessandro followed the paths of single swallows in steep arcs rocketing upward or in descent. How quick they were to turn when turning was in order, or to roll and dart through

groups of birds fired at them, as if from a cannon, in an exploding star. This they did of their own volition, and they did it again and again.

For Alessandro they were the unification of risk and hope. It is hard to track them in violent winds high in the blue where they seem to disappear into the color itself, but as long as they take their great chances in the air, as long as they swoop in flights that bring them close to death, you cannot tell if, having risen, they will plummet, or, having plummeted, they will rise.

A story like this demands the lyricism with which Helprin infuses it; a stingier description would neither tell the same tale nor reveal the same character.

At the other end of the continuum are the short stories of Raymond Carver. His prose is quiet, stark, and studded with small, exquisitely chosen details—a descriptive style that matches his somber stories about the terror and pathos of ordinary lives. In "Nobody Said Anything," the narrator—whose irritable, exhausted parents are on the brink of splitting up—observes his mother leaving for work in her white blouse and black skirt:

> . . . Sometimes she called it her outfit, sometimes her uniform. For as long as I could remember, it was always hanging in the closet or hanging on the clothesline or getting washed out by hand at night or being ironed in the kitchen.

Not an adjective in the whole passage, and yet Carver paints an accurate, vibrant picture of the boy's mother, informing the readers about how the boy views her and what their life together is like.

In the novels of Anne Tyler you will find a descriptive style that falls somewhere between these two extremes. Tyler's characters are unusual, often eccentric, and yet utterly real. She makes them real through description that is, like all good description, accurate and relevant. In an early scene from *The Accidental Tourist,* Macon is observing Muriel, "hoping for flaws." The word "hoping" is key here, for Macon does not want to fall for Muriel, or anyone. He does find flaws, described this way:

> . . . a long, narrow nose, and sallow skin, and two freckled knobs of collarbone that promised an unluxurious body.

Macon's view of Muriel's nose and skin might lead readers to believe he is not attracted to her, but the "freckled knobs of collarbone" give him away, a detail that shows Muriel to be both vulnerable and endearing. This is an accurate portrayal of Muriel—she is indeed a bony woman—but also a relevant one, for Macon is exactly the person who could take a meticulous physical inventory of someone and not realize what he is really seeing.

Whether you fall on the baroque or puritan end of the description continuum or somewhere in between, remember that description is not a separate technique that decorates a story; it is a variety of techniques that combine to make a story. After the joyful rush of the first draft, these decisions must be consciously reviewed. Are my details accurate? Did I use the right point of view? Did I use too much narrative and not enough scene? Is my dialogue realistic? Does the flashback create a full enough portrait of the character's childhood? Is my style too ornate for this simple setting? Is the pace too slow or too fast? Are my metaphors overdone? All these questions go straight to the heart of description.

As you read through this book you will be reminded again and again that good description does not flow naturally from the pen. All writers, no matter how experienced, must consciously and purposefully attend to the techniques that make up description. In the following chapters I will explain these techniques—for example, the telling detail, dialogue, point of view, scene, narrative, and flashback—and offer you different ways to use them. By studying these techniques and applying them to your own work, you will come to understand how critical these techniques are for creating rich mental images, for turning a story from an account of something to a description of something. As every writer knows, writing can be by turns thrilling and delightful, discouraging and cheerless. What better antidote for those occasions of discouragement than the discovery of brand-new fiction-writing tools!

CHAPTER 1

DETAILS, DETAILS

DETAILS, AT LEAST THE KIND that make fiction live, can be as small as a well-placed adjective and as large as a central metaphor. Beginning students often scratch their heads when told their stories lack detail. Didn't they point out that the heroine possessed an "interesting personality"? Isn't that a detail? Well, yes and no. It's a detail, but not a useful one. A "calamitous personality," maybe; the "personality of a bee trapped in a mason jar"—now we're talking detail. A detail is a word or phrase or image that helps the readers "see." Don't tell your readers that Judy "looked sad," tell us about the shape of her mouth or the lifeless slats of her hair. Avoid details that call to mind *anybody* and use the ones that call to mind *somebody*.

THE TELLING DETAIL

Sometimes it takes only one or two details to light up a character for your readers. These precise, illuminating finds are the "telling" details of fiction, for they stretch beyond mere observation to give the readers a larger, richer sense of character or place. The old man's carefully parted hair suggests that he has not totally given up. The tinny clatter of cheap crockery implies that the restaurateur has fallen on hard times. The sullen teenager's one-shouldered shrug connotes indifference tinged with contempt.

This kind of detail makes fiction more than what-happens-next storytelling. It makes description more than an account. The right details, inserted at the right times, allow your readers access to a character's inner landscape, to his or her peculiarities, fears, and compulsions that cannot be easily explained. It is one thing to explain to your readers that a character is fearful, quite another to describe the way she shrinks from human touch.

Imagine that you are writing a story about a shy, middle-aged man named Frankie. All his life Frankie has been sheltered by his mother, who has recently died. Your story is about Frankie's struggle to define a life for himself. Picking up the story about two weeks into Frankie's plight, you could begin this way:

> Everything was his now: the bank account, his mother's apartment on Lexington, the fake mantel on which her heart-breaking shepherdess figurines went about their work.

Notice how the telling details in this opening sentence work together. In the first part of the sentence, we are introduced to someone whose mother has died and left some conventional things—money and an apartment. With only these details, we don't know how Frankie feels about his loss; for all we know he could have killed the old lady himself. But the sentence goes on to describe the fake mantel and the shepherdess figurines, "telling" details that soften the harsh introduction of property and money. We get a sense of an orderly apartment in which life was gentle. We have all seen those figurines, in the parlors of our grandmothers or in the windows of the five-and-dime. The way those figurines are described gives us two insights. One: that the shepherdesses are "heartbreaking" implies that Frankie is himself heartbroken; two: that the shepherdesses are going "about their work" implies that Frankie understands, however unconsciously, that he, too, must go on. In one opening line you have given your readers a setting, a character, and an attitude. You have opened the door not to a story, but to an entire world.

Openings like this one depend on your attention to detail. This attention requires careful work that often means paring an entire paragraph to one sentence. After you delete all the mundane, irrelevant information, you might have very little left and have to start again from scratch. The lazy way into this story would read something like this:

> Frankie's mother had died two weeks ago, leaving him ev-

erything she owned. He was heartbroken and scared, knowing he would miss his mother and the gentle life he'd led inside the walls of her orderly little apartment on Lexington. Yet on some level he realized that life must go on.

Do you see how much vitality you've lost by offering information rather than detail?

HOW DETAILS DRIVE THE STORY

At certain junctures, especially in a first draft, you may stumble across a detail that is so telling to *you* that it changes the direction of your story. After giving the readers a bit more about Frankie and his circumstances, let's say you decide to send him to the library, where he sees Andrea, the assistant librarian whom he's long admired from afar. He selects a book from the stacks and prepares to take it to the circulation desk. Which book? Here is the next telling detail. What if he checks out *Oliver Twist*? What about *How to Plant a Flower Garden*? What about *Oriental Sex Secrets*? For reasons you don't fully recognize yet yourself, you decide that *How to Plant a Flower Garden* is Frankie's choice. At this point it simply *feels* right. This choice is important not only because it reveals something about Frankie, but because it dictates where the story is going next.

Recognizing the junctures at which the telling detail is important will help you not only to write in crisp, evocative prose, but also to define your story. How do you recognize these junctures? Unfortunately, there are no rules for intuition, but you might notice that telling details crop up most often when the description addresses itself to one of two areas: a character's immediate surroundings or a character's decision to do something. Certainly the description of Frankie's mother's apartment (the character's immediate surroundings) engages the readers not with a character named Frankie, but with a *certain kind* of character named Frankie. Similarly, Frankie's choice of books (the character's decision to do something) allows the story to take not only a turn, but a *certain kind* of turn. If Frankie puts the garden book back on the shelf and takes the sex book instead, then your story has to head down a different path altogether. And if the story had opened with a description of bars on the windows instead of shepherdesses on the mantel, you would have an entirely different Frankie to work with.

The Frankie you have to contend with now, however, is not concerned with bars on windows. He is nervous about checking the book out himself; his mother had always performed this task for him. You can describe his discomfort in many ways. For starters, you can come right out and tell the readers what Frankie is feeling:

> Frankie wasn't even sure how to go about checking out a book. Was his library card still current? How much would he have to say? Perhaps he could get away with smiling his way through it; his mother always said his smile was darling.

The interior monologue ("Was his library card still current . . .") is nice, and as good a way as any to describe what Frankie is feeling. It's not until the final line, however, that we get the jolt of recognition that comes with just the right detail. That Frankie, a middle-aged man, is comforted by remembering that his mother always thought his smile was "darling" tells us volumes about his helplessness, his dependency, and his too-close relationship with his mother. You might try a little of that same subtlety in the sentences leading up to that final revelation:

> Frankie took his place at the back of the line and set his eyes on the fellow in front of him. A nice-looking boy (college student, Frankie decided), shirt collar turned up, jeans ripped fashionably at the knee. His three books, held casually against one hip, seemed stylish somehow, part of the outfit. Frankie watched him with the precision of a cat as the line dwindled, bringing him nearer to Andrea. Finally it was the boy's turn; he exchanged a few pleasantries with Andrea, his words not so much spoken as poured. Frankie turned to the woman behind him and offered her his place, then waited once again at the line's end, squinting under the harsh fluorescent light. Maybe he could simply smile through the transaction. His mother always said his smile was darling.

This version is longer, but more precise. In the first version the details are few and all we know is that Frankie is generally worried about speaking to Andrea. In the second, you invent someone for Frankie to compare himself to, and the way Frankie views this boy is very telling. By describing how the college kid looks, you are also implying that Frankie must look exactly the opposite, and also that Frankie sees him as competition for Andrea's interest. Here's a twist you hadn't thought of until you began to describe the college boy in the kind of detail that reflects back on Frankie. Also, the observation that the boy's words seem "poured" lets us in on Frankie's fear of how his own words will sound. Perhaps Frankie has a good reason for not wanting to speak? An accent? A stutter? You're learning something about a character of your own invention as your careful details carry you forward. Revelations of this kind become more common as your powers of observation become more precise.

Like most writers, you probably begin a first draft with only a general idea of what is going to happen. The telling detail can be your compass, your way of navigating through a story, guiding your character down one path at the expense of another. Let's say you're writing a story about a lonely office worker who adopts a litter of puppies. While you're describing your main character, out pops a description of her hair, "so silver it looks cold." You like it—but you've got a problem: a woman with cold hair doesn't sound like the puppy-loving type. Therefore the litter of puppies you've left at her office door poses a dilemma quite different from the one you originally envisioned. The story was going to be about a woman's struggle to keep seven puppies; now the story is going to be about a woman's struggle to get rid of seven puppies. The telling detail is a joy to the appreciative reader, but to you, the writer, it is also a valuable doorway through which you enter the mysterious inner chambers of your own characters' lives.

ADDING DETAILS IN LATER DRAFTS

Telling details appear in two ways: suddenly, from your unconscious, to tell you what you need to know about your characters; and deliberately, from your conscious writing self, who already knows the character very well and must divine the most vivid way to convey that knowledge to the readers.

How do you deliberately create a telling detail? In our story about Frankie, many telling details came to us suddenly, and dictated the course of the story. This is what happens in first drafts. In later drafts, however, after we have a good idea of who the character is and the shape of the story in which we have placed him, we should look around for places where a telling detail could enrich the prose. Suppose the first draft contains a scene in the apartment just after Frankie has come home from the library. He gets a glass of milk and sits down at the kitchen table with the book. He begins to leaf through the book, marvelling at the magnificent floral specimens. The scene, as written, contains some rich imagery, including pictures of flowers that seem to furl out from the damp pages, and drops of milk sliding along the side of the glass as Frankie sets it down.

Very nice. But wrong, you decide, in retrospect. At this point in the story, Frankie is still in a cocoon; he has not yet decided to do anything about his life. He cannot yet see the possibilities in flowers. The imagery should be dry, not wet. Get rid of the milk. Put him in the parlor instead of the kitchen, and describe the dusty sunlight coming through the windows. Describe the chalky sound of his weight shifting in the chair. The pictures in the book are flat, not furled. Frankie doesn't yet have the imagination to see real flowers from these pictures. The pages are dry, not damp. Perhaps the sound of his fingers on the pages sounds a little like mice in the walls.

Telling detail is part inspiration and part determination. Keep reminding yourself (in the later drafts) what your story is really about, what phases of human understanding your character is passing through, and create the details accordingly.

ENGAGING THE SENSES

In your rush to get an early draft committed to paper, you could be relying too much on the visual aspects of description. Even your "telling" details are probably visual ones: a shard of mirror, a twisted lamppost, a blue eyelid. *Remember, you have four other senses to work with: taste, touch, smell, and sound.* What your character smells and hears may be even more important than what he sees. A festooned riverboat (a feast for the eyes) might be easy and fun to describe, but the metallic taste in the captain's mouth or the sulphurous odor of the water may be more important to the story.

Look again at the "lazy" beginning from our story about Frankie:

Frankie's mother had died two weeks ago, leaving him everything she owned. He was heartbroken and scared, knowing he would miss his mother and the gentle life he'd led inside the walls of her orderly little apartment on Lexington. Yet on some level he realized that life must go on.

This passage suffers from more than just a lack of telling detail; did you notice that not *one* of the senses appears here? Frankie—and the reader—hears nothing, smells nothing, tastes nothing, feels nothing, and sees nothing, unless you count the general visual impression suggested by the "orderly" apartment.

Let's continue with Frankie's story as we explore ways of improving description by using sensory details. Frankie checks out his book on flower gardening without saying a word to Andrea. (Let's decide that he does have a stutter.) Humiliated, he slinks out of the library with the book tucked under his arm like something he has stolen.

As it turns out, Frankie *does* end up stealing the book, because he loves it so much and is too shy to return to the library to renew it. He ignores the overdue notices as he spends his spring and summer creating a garden on the patio of his mother's apartment. By August, there comes a moment when Frankie learns something about gardening:

Frankie studied the bare spots in his garden, perplexed. Except for a stunning pair of day lilies that he'd been assured would grow anyplace, nothing was blooming. The bursts of magenta and blue he'd been counting on since April were nowhere to be found. The delphiniums and hollyhocks—whose showstopping blossoms he'd been drawn to in the book—were pathetic little sprigs. He glanced up at the weak city sun and realized his mistake: The "full sun" described by the book had never shone on him.

The foregoing passage is adequate for describing Frankie's puzzlement, but a quick scan reveals a missed opportunity. The setting is a *garden*, for goodness sake, and yet the passage engages none of the senses except the sense of sight. Try this one again, using more sensory detail:

Frankie dug into the soil, breathing its damp aroma. He shaped his fingers around the delphiniums' stunted roots, then sat back, perplexed. Except for a pair of ordinary day lilies that rustled near the railing, nothing was blooming. The delphiniums that had caught his eye on the dry pages of his library book had grown only a few inches, a wizened row of sprigs. Below him, the clamor of the morning commute began in the street, exhaust fumes rising. Frankie squinted up at a weak strand of sunlight muscling its way through the grainy air, just enough of a glimmer to warm his balding head. Wiping his hands on his shirt, he realized his mistake: The "full sun" described by the book had never shone on him.

Notice how the sensory details enrich this passage. The competing sounds in this passage—rustling lilies and morning traffic—contain intimations of both hope and despair. Similarly, the garden's damp scent and the feel of sun on Frankie's forehead are signs of hope that offset the despair of the stunted plants and the city's grainy air. This passage is full of atmosphere that illuminates not only Frankie's bewilderment, but his fragile position. He can follow the promise of his garden (the lilies, the rich soil) or succumb to its failure (weak sunlight, exhaust fumes, pathetic sprigs). Instead of information about Frankie, we now have insights about Frankie, for sensory details are evocative, suggestive, telling. And because we've been seduced into sensing Frankie's world, we now have a stake in how he chooses to move through it. The final line presents a challenge: Will Frankie come down on the side of hope ("full sun") or despair ("never shone on him")?

Sensory details invite readers to take your character's side, to understand what is happening to him, to empathize with his every hope and fear. These details bring breadth and depth to character and setting, informing your readers in ways that are surprising, revealing, and a pleasure to read.

SIMILE AND METAPHOR

The strong imagery contained in simile and metaphor is the blood and guts of descriptive fiction. Without it you are working with a mere skeleton, telling rather than showing. Used well, simile and metaphor bring prose to life; paradoxically, however, its overuse can smother the prose and bury the story.

A simile is a figure of speech, usually introduced by *like* or *as*, that compares one thing to another:

> Emmett is as relentless as a wolverine.
> Jenny's eyes shine like chips of onyx.

Because a simile's sole function is comparison, it is not quite as evocative as a metaphor. A metaphor does not so much compare as *transform* one thing to another:

> Luanne was a dainty little bird of a woman, given to quick movements.
> Behind the house Feldman laid out four squadrons of flowers that sprouted, mute and soldierly, exactly where he had planted them.

Metaphor is subtler and more revealing than simile, evoking imagery beyond the original comparison. Luanne is transformed into a bird, with all the attendant (and unmentioned) fluff and chatter and skittishness that we associate with birds. Feldman's squadrons of flowers suggest something about Feldman himself, evoking military associations and the sense that Feldman always gets exactly what he demands.

With a simile, the comparison stops at the end of the sentence; with a metaphor, the reader's imagination goes on to include all the images and associations that the metaphor implies.

Sometimes you can convert a prosaic simile into a vivid metaphor:

> **Simile:** Emmett is as relentless as a wolverine.
> **Metaphor:** "Emmett?" Judy said. "Emmett is nothing but a wolverine, hateful and relentless. Sometimes at night I think I hear him out there, panting at the edge of the yard."

The metaphor transforms Emmett from a man who reminds somebody of a wolverine into a man who embodies the wolverine's terrifying qualities and who evokes the resulting fear and loathing.

A metaphor can resonate far beyond its original invocation; you can thread a metaphor all the way through a story if you want to. An insistent rain might fall through a story about a failed businesswoman trying to get back on her feet. This kind of recurring imagery is a story's *central metaphor*. For example, you could fashion a story around an ice-climbing expedition, using it to mirror and vivify the up-and-down emotions that the climber is experiencing in his crumbling marriage. Michelangelo's *Pietà* could be the central metaphor in a story about a woman artist tending her own dying son.

Writers often discover central metaphors by accident. A friend might exclaim, "I love the kite-flying as a metaphor for Kate's marriage," leaving us to nod wisely while secretly wondering how we ever missed it. Much of our writing comes from the subconscious, and we are all guided by our own personal metaphors, which is why some authors seem to write the same novels over and over. Make yourself aware of your own recurring metaphors, and be careful not to let them become stale.

Whether you discover a central metaphor by accident, or deliberately set out to create one, make sure to weave it subtly into the body of the story, and keep it free of cliché. For example, a five-page story about a young girl's coming of age may be smothered by too many images of springtime, making a simple story seem overblown and melodramatic: blooming flowers, blooming girl. Just because you find some recurring images while rereading a first draft does not mean you are obliged to turn those images into a central metaphor. You may even want to cut some of the images and let the story stand a little more by itself.

Let's return for the moment to our story about Frankie. Notice that a central metaphor is beginning to show itself: light. The harsh fluorescent light of the library; the weak strand of sunlight on his bald head; the observation that full sun has never shone on him. Once you discover a pattern like this, you have a decision to make: punch it up, or tone it down. In this case, the central metaphor of light suits your purpose for Frankie, and you can punch it up a bit by altering Frankie's appearance. Instead of a bald head, give him a stalk of unruly, flame-orange hair that embarrasses him almost as much as his stutter. When the sun shines on him he looks like a lighted match. The recurring image of light in this story is a metaphor for the darkness of Frankie's life, for he has never truly ventured out into the sun. The scene where he is kneeling in his garden with the sun shining on him is a powerful one, inviting the suggestion that Frankie is like the flowers he has planted. Will he blossom like the "ordinary" day lilies, or wither like the delphiniums, which were more promising on paper than in reality?

Let's give Frankie a break and write him a happy ending. He decides he isn't made for raising showy flowers; he doesn't have the right conditions (literally and metaphorically, of course). However, he knows he can grow easy flowers, as proved by the day lilies, so he fills his barren garden with them, discovering how beautiful they are when massed together. As a final act of faith, he gathers the most beautiful of the lilies and heads back to the library to return the book to Andrea. The story ends with Frankie standing in front of the library first thing in the morning, waiting for Andrea to unlock the door. This final moment cries out for a strong image; after all, Frankie has decided to allow the full sun to shine on him at last:

> Frankie stood at the library door, flowers in one hand and book in the other, his hair brushed into the red pompadour of a rooster about to announce the dawn.

This final metaphor (the rooster) illuminates Frankie's awkward confidence (his wild red hair has been turned into an asset) and his decision to begin anew. Moreover, "announcing the dawn" brings in a final, reassuring image of light.

THE VIRTUE OF RESTRAINT

Simile and metaphor are irresistible writing devices, but you must take care to control your impulses. We writers are always seeing things in terms of something else (it's called imagination) but imagery can become so burdensome that the readers can't find the story. Metaphors look obvious and simple-minded if rendered too directly and too frequently. Images like thunderclaps during the sex scene, or wolves howling on the evening before the execution are best left behind. And beware of mixed metaphors, in which imagery runs away with itself and ends up confusing the readers:

> Arianna shook back her mane of auburn hair. She began

to slink toward me, a lioness with the single-mindedness of a rattlesnake.

Are you comparing Arianna with a lion or a snake? Once you've begun with one image (the "mane of hair" already suggests a lion), don't mar it by adding something else. It can be fun, however, to allow your characters themselves to mix metaphors. The character who proclaims "You can't make a gift horse out of a sow's ear" makes for entertaining company.

WRAP-UP

The next time you set out to write a story, remember how versatile the telling detail can be. One well-placed detail can save you half a page of description. Telling details can be come upon accidentally in the rush of a first draft, or they can be deliberately crafted, puzzled over, and inserted into places where either your character or plot requires a certain kind of image: timidity (a fleeing mouse, half-drawn shades); corruption (broken-up asphalt, fishnet stockings); hope (apple orchards, new shingles). These details are the "way in" to the story, and the readers will appreciate them.

Details are not merely visual; remember to engage all the senses. The dryness of chalk on the fingers can be more arresting than the visual image of a character's whitened fingertips. Sounds and scents and tastes also add to a reader's engagement with the story.

Simile and metaphor make fiction breathe. Simile, which is a figure of speech comparing one thing with another, can help readers "see" what you're describing. Beware of its overuse, lest you be accused of trying too hard to be writerly. Metaphor is subtler than simile, because it does not compare so much as transform. A little girl becomes a kitten when described in terms of feline mewing and skittish motion. Metaphors can be contained in one sentence, or expanded to thread through an entire story as a central metaphor. A snowstorm, a railroad, or a pair of red shoes are images that could be expanded into metaphors for confusion, progress, or heedlessness.

The telling detail is where description begins. It is the device through which you introduce your readers—and sometimes yourself—to the true nature of your characters.

CHAPTER 2

SHOWING AND TELLING

SHOW-DON'T-TELL, SHOW-DON'T-TELL, show-don't-tell. Wherever you go—writing conferences, university classrooms, writers' groups—you hear this well-used writing maxim. "Showing" is generally thought of as using vivid details and engaging the senses, therefore painting a bright descriptive picture for the readers: the richness of a landscape, the shock of disappointment in a new marriage, the fireworks of rage between Character A and Character B. "Telling" is generally thought of as the absence of vivid detail—uninspired narrative that serves only to explain what is going on in the story: who is related to whom, where the town is located, how Character C got her nickname, and so on.

Neither of these characterizations is entirely correct. "Show, don't tell" is a *guideline,* not a rule! "Showing" can indeed reveal character and plot in a dynamic way. However, "telling" can often do the same thing as long as you find the right words. Showing and telling are equally powerful and important descriptive techniques. Before we explore their possibilities, let's review their differences.

WHAT'S THE DIFFERENCE?

Showing and telling are the heart and soul of description, but many inexperienced writers have trouble discerning the difference between them. The following example should give you a fair idea of how these techniques differ. Imagine you've created a mousy little

18

character named Alice, whom you introduce through the technique of "telling":

> **Version One—Telling:** Alice was a timid young woman who looked like a mouse. She was short and skinny, with brown hair, small eyes, and a pointed face. She always peeked inside the doorway before entering a party, thus giving herself a chance to flee in case she saw no one she knew.

Now try this introduction again, this time using the technique of "showing":

> **Version Two—Showing:** Alice hovered at the door of Everett's apartment, chin lifted, tiny feet balanced on their toes. She peered inside, shrinking at the loudness of Everett's new stereo. She breathed quickly, her black eyes darting back and forth, as if keeping her face in motion might prevent her from toppling over. When she finally spotted the wide-grinning Everett approaching, she scurried to the punch bowl, her flat shoes making a scritching sound on the polished wood.

In Version One, you tell the readers that Alice looks and acts like a mouse; in Version Two, you show her in mouselike terms: black eyes, quivering face, tiptoed stance, scritching sound.

Each version is serviceable enough, but each also comes with potential problems. In Version One, the description of Alice is accurate but perfunctory: timid, short, brown hair, small eyes. The passage picks up a little with the image of her "peeking" inside the doorway, then loses steam again with a plodding explanation: "thus giving her a chance to flee . . ." The readers can't really "see" Alice here. You are pausing to tell them something about Alice in order for the next part of the story to make more sense. When Alice finally walks into the party and hides behind a potted plant, the readers understand that she's doing this because she is timid and mouselike. This explanation is fine, for now; you have not necessarily made a mistake in telling the readers what Alice looks like. But if subsequent descriptions take the same form (Reginald was tall and grim and looked like a goose; Evelyn looked like a plucked chicken and had a temperament to match), your prose is going to start seeming flat and expository. You're explaining too much up front, rather than letting the characters reveal themselves through their words and deeds. The readers will feel as if they're watching characters on a screen, or leafing through photographs of characters, rather than entering the story and inhabiting the characters' world.

In Version Two, on the other hand, you allow the readers into Alice's world. We can feel Alice's nervousness because of the motion and sound in the description: she darts and hovers and scritches and shrinks. Again, there is nothing wrong with this passage. In fact, it portrays Alice so vividly that we can easily imagine ourselves at the door of the party with her. The caution with this kind of showing is not to overdo it. Depending on what happens next in the story, you may be lingering too long at the door. Maybe Alice isn't the main character, and all this "showing" is taking the spotlight away from someone else who is more important. Besides, too much showing can start to seem self-conscious, as if you're brandishing your arsenal of similes and metaphors just for the heck of it. Your characters might even disappear in the process. Don't let your prose style overwhelm the story you want to tell.

Too much telling can flatten your story, too much showing can overwhelm it. What's a conscientious writer to do? A combination of showing and telling usually yields the best description:

> **Combination:** Alice stood at the door of Everett's apartment with all the self-possession of a field mouse. Hands clasped at the waist, she stood on tiptoe and peered inside to see who she might know.

The reason the combination works so much better is that a little bit of telling makes the showing seem less labored. By coming right out with the mouse analogy at the beginning, you can give Alice's mouse-like qualities a more subtle turn; the phrase "all the self-possession of a field mouse" suggest lots of other mouselike qualities: skittishness, vigilance, furtiveness. You don't have to "show" every one of them. A couple of small touches—clasped hands, tiptoed stance—paints a nearly complete picture. Don't deny your readers the pleasure of filling in some details themselves.

Examine the work of your most cherished authors, and you will find that the show-tell combination permeates their best stories. To admonish writers to show and not tell is to rob them of the deep satisfaction of learning to balance these wonderful techniques.

SCENE AND NARRATIVE

The above examples illustrate showing and telling only in their most general application. In their most technical form, showing can be thought of as *scene*, telling as *narrative*. To properly balance scene and narrative so that a story takes on depth and insight and rhythm and shape, you must first understand the difference between scene and narrative and how they complement each other.

Scene serves a specific purpose; it usually contains dialogue; it has a beginning, middle, and end; and it moves the story forward. *Narrative* is the flow of prose—the string of sentences and paragraphs— that tell the story. A scene almost always contains some narrative, but the converse is not true; narrative does not have to contain scene.

Let's begin a story in two ways, first with a narrative passage and then with a short scene.

> **Narrative ("telling"):** Ms. Kendall was Middleton School's most popular teacher. She was always bringing in maps and atlases to brighten her classroom and motivate her fourth graders. The children adored her and ran to her aid every time they had a chance. Mrs. Brimley, the other fourth-grade teacher, watched this daily homage with a mixture of resentment and awe.

As you can see from the above passage, narrative allows you to make the point and do the informing yourself. You can give readers direct information about your characters' virtues, failings, and inner conflicts as well as the more mundane aspects of their lives: employment, appearance, or marital status, for example.

In a scene, on the other hand, the characters and setting can make the point for you:

> **Scene ("showing"):** Ms. Kendall paused at her classroom door and shifted her full-color maps of the NATO nations from one arm to the other. Spotting her, a small group of fourth graders dropped the books they were hauling and rushed to her aid, yipping like puppies, each clamoring to be the one to turn the knob.
>
> "Children! Children!" Ms. Kendall trilled, her musical laughter echoing down the dingy corridor. "One at a time, now. You can't all help at once."

Mrs. Brimley, marooned at the far end of the hall amidst a splatter of upended math books, thinned her lips and sighed over the echo of stampeding feet.

This passage, though brief, can be considered a scene because it serves a purpose (to show that Ms. Kendall is popular with the children and that Mrs. Brimley resents it); it contains dialogue; it has a beginning (the pause at the door), a middle (the stampede), and an end (Mrs. Brimley's abandonment); and it moves the story forward (puts Mrs. Brimley in a position of reacting to what she has just experienced). Mini-scenes like this combine to create larger scenes, and the larger scenes combine to create a story. Scenes have to be relieved by spots of narrative, though, or your story will never end. For example, a narrative passage like this—"Mrs. Brimley marched the children through their multiplication drills, willing the clock's heavy hands to move"—saves you a long, unnecessary scene depicting Mrs. Brimley drilling her students. You can suggest the torpor of the long afternoon without subjecting the unfortunate readers to a torpid scene.

Most of us have been trained to think of narrative (telling) as "bad description" and scene (showing) as "good description." Certainly a case can be made that in the above examples, the scene is better than the narrative passage, but that's only because both passages are rendered in such extremes. The narrative passage is dull and expository—it doesn't vividly describe the Kendall-Brimley conflict. The verbs aren't particularly strong (was; motivate; ran; watched), and the picture being painted doesn't engage the senses. There is no sound or movement; again, we're watching characters on a screen. The scene, on the other hand, contains noise and movement and dialogue and marvelous verbs like "marooned" and "yipping." Does that mean you should begin this story with a scene? Not necessarily.

Perhaps you wish to paint only a brief (but potent) picture of the Brimley-Kendall relationship to get to the real story, which is about Mrs. Brimley. Perhaps you plan to portray Mrs. Brimley as a woman with numerous personal burdens—a dying mother, a divorce in progress, fading beauty, an ungrateful son—who becomes fascinated by Ms. Kendall, in whom she sees the girl she herself once was. In a rare impulsive moment Mrs. Brimley steals Ms. Kendall's classroom key. She begins to prowl Ms. Kendall's classroom at night, sifting through Ms. Kendall's button collection and cuddling the classroom hamster. In time she can't stop, for Ms. Kendall's possessions have become talismans of sorts, good-luck charms that fend off Mrs. Brimley's weariness and grief. If this is the story you decide to tell, then the above scene might not merit so much ado; you might want to deliver the initial information quickly, in order to get on with the real story. Back to narrative, then—but this time with more attention to the prose:

> **Narrative, second draft:** Mrs. Brimley envied Ms. Kendall's youth: her silky arms, her just-washed hair, her easy way with the thirty-five fourth graders they divided between them. The children preferred Ms. Kendall, every last one of them, and who could blame them? She had the voice of an angel; her laughter was a salve. *I love her,* Mrs. Brimley whispered dozens of times a day. *And I hate her.*

Do you see the difference? This is narrative that is every bit as effective as scene. Narrative does not have to be merely informational. This passage contains imagistic language ("silky arms" and laughter like a "salve") and a haunting bit of sound with the whispered "I love her . . . I hate her." The internal monologue (". . . who could blame them?") brings your readers deep inside Mrs. Brimley's experience.

Now you have an engaging story opening that introduces two contrasting characters and sets up a tense internal conflict in Mrs. Brimley. Technically, you have "shown" nothing, but by using imagistic language and a bit of internal monologue you have summarized the story's basic conflict and given your lucky readers a perfect point of entry: a character with some meat on her bones, and a story with a destination. You have revealed something about Mrs. Brimley that might have been diluted or lost in a full-blown scene.

If you forced yourself to "show" everything you've "told" in this passage, you'd be confronted with five pages instead of one paragraph. You'd have to begin with a scene that shows Ms. Kendall being the preferred teacher, then you'd have to show Mrs. Brimley in a situation where she loves Ms. Kendall, and another in which she hates her. You'd lose the immediacy of the dilemma, the mantra-like

I love her, I hate her, the tinge of mystery, and the intensity of Mrs. Brimley's sorrow. A scene-by-scene revelation would rob your readers of that exquisite, all-at-once wallop of insight—that Mrs. Brimley has suffered a long time with her conflicting emotions. Besides, your readers may become impatient with a story that takes too long to begin.

Of course, the happiest compromise in the scene-narrative dilemma is combination. This blending process is what good writing is all about. During revision you make continual decisions about scene and narrative, whether you realize it or not. You might throw out a line here, add a snippet of dialogue there, change an adjective or verb. You're balancing, balancing: scene and narrative, narrative and scene. Showing, telling, telling, showing. The combination often yields something like the following:

> **Combination narrative and scene:** Mrs. Brimley's 4A's, each with an armload of math books they were helping to transfer from the library to Room 3, spotted Ms. Kendall at the other end of the corridor. She was stalled at her classroom door, shifting her own bundle—full-color maps of the NATO nations—from one arm to the other. Dropping their books like so many bombs, the 4A's rushed to her aid, yipping like puppies, each clamoring to be the one to turn the knob.
>
> "Children! Children!" Ms. Kendall trilled, her musical laughter echoing down the dingy corridor. "One at a time, now. You can't all help at once."
>
> Mrs. Brimley, suddenly marooned amidst a splatter of up-ended books, thinned her lips and sighed over the echo of stampeding feet. She envied Ms. Kendall's youth: her silky arms, her just-washed hair, her easy way with the children. Who could blame them for adoring her? She had the voice of an angel; her laughter was a salve. Mrs. Brimley sighed, bending to retrieve the books. *I hate her,* she whispered, tucking back a ripped page. *And I love her.*

This blend of narrative and scene yields a meaty, intriguing opening for your story. Scene and narrative do not always have to be combined, however. You may have a stylistic preference for one over the other; your intentions for the story may require more narrative than scene, or vice versa. Some stories can successfully be rendered as scene alone—completely in dialogue and gesture, with no narrative at all. Other excellent stories are told entirely as narrative in which no dialogue intrudes and the prose flows smoothly from beginning to end. In general, though, a combination of scene and narrative makes for the most pleasing and traditional storytelling.

HOW TO "TELL"

Readers (and writing instructors) won't complain that you're "telling too much" as long as your prose sings. Whether you choose a folk song or an aria is up to you. Some telling can be downright showy and makes for splendid description. Look at the differences in the following simple, declarative sentences:

> Mrs. Brimley went into Ms. Kendall's classroom.
> Mrs. Brimley sneaked into Ms. Kendall's classroom.
> Mrs. Brimley lurched into Ms. Kendall's classroom.

All three sentences describe a person entering a room. Can you see how much less vivid the first one is than the others? Remember, no matter how small the action, you are *describing* it to the readers, not just informing them that it happened. You can add life to a sentence just by changing the verb. Verbs like "sneaked" or "lurched" suggest more than a mere action; they describe a character's state of mind. Embroider the sentence even further, with some strong images, and the prose springs to life:

> Mrs. Brimley sneaked into the darkened classroom, her breath stalled in her throat, her eyes caught on a slender thread of moonlight that defined the wire rungs of the hamster's cage.

This is a good example of a narrative passage that gets its energy from imagistic language. Not only are you telling your readers that Mrs. Brimley is entering the classroom on the sly, you are showing them her heightened sense of awareness by describing the light on the cage. You are also showing them that Mrs. Brimley's clandestine entry is at night without ever coming right out and saying "that night," or "long after dark." The thread of moonlight tells the tale. You can go on to describe the creases in Mrs. Brimley's face, the hair that's mashed down on one side, the glint of her mother's ring under the eerie light. Technically, you're still telling, but in a way that offers the readers a vivid picture of a woman who is not altogether grounded, at least not at the moment. Call it "show-telling" if you wish. Show-telling demonstrates your descriptive powers. No one will fault you for that. Readers complain, "It's too talky" or "Nothing's happened yet" only when the prose itself is flat.

Another way to get a "showy" quality into your narrative is to use internal monologue. Internal monologue is a narrative line that is intended to echo the character's own voice. It is a very effective way to bring the readers so close to the character's experience that they feel they are being "shown" the character's innermost thoughts. Look at the following narrative passage, which uses no internal monologue:

> **Straight narrative:** Mrs. Brimley skulked the perimeter of Ms. Kendall's classroom, allowing her eyes to adjust to the dark. Slowly the shapes of the classroom came clear: desks moved into groupings of four; a full-sized skeleton propped on its stand; silhouettes of posters and bookcases. The aquarium cast an eerie light across the back of the room, where Ms. Kendall's calico hamster ran round and round the wheel in its cage. Her heart seemed to beat in concert with that whirring wheel, for she felt guilty for leaving her mother alone and began to worry that something had happened in her absence. And yet she could not leave. Entering this classroom, this mysterious, underlit realm, made her feel so close to Ms. Kendall.

This is a perfectly functional "tell" passage that uses some good, imagistic language. Still, you are "telling" an awful lot: how Mrs. Brimley feels (guilty and worried), what the room looks like, why she won't leave (she feels close to Ms. Kendall). In the following revision, internal monologue enlivens the passage a bit, bringing readers so close to Mrs. Brimley's experience that the passage seems to "show" more than "tell," even though it retains its narrative character:

> **Internal monologue added:** Mrs. Brimley skulked the perimeter of Ms. Kendall's classroom, allowing her eyes to adjust to the dark. How beautifully the shapes appeared: desks in happy groupings, the classroom skeleton loitering on its stand; posters

and bookcases poised in silhouette! The aquarium cast an eerie light across the back of the room, where Ms. Kendall's calico hamster ran round and round the wheel in its cage. Like my heart, Mrs. Brimley thought, putting a hand on her chest. She felt it beating in concert with that whirring wheel. She had left her mother alone, but who could fault her? Who could blame her for lingering in this mysterious, underlit realm, this place that felt like the inside of her own soul?

Okay, maybe it gets a little melodramatic at the end, but can you see the way the internal monologue works to "show" what Mrs. Brimley is experiencing? It is as if Mrs. Brimley is speaking directly to us. Her voice emerges obscurely at first: *How beautifully the shapes appeared!*; then more prominently: *Like my heart, Mrs. Brimley thought*; and then we hear the echo of her literal voice: . . . *who could fault her? Who could blame her* . . . ? It's as if she is saying, Who could fault me? Who could blame me . . . ? Internal monologue, more than any other technique, blurs the line between scene and narrative, because the dialogue of a scene is implied within the narrative.

As you can see, telling doesn't exist in one box, showing in another. If the prose is rich and careful, showing and telling become inseparable.

HOW TO "SHOW"

Inexperienced writers often take "showing" to extremes. They believe that good description means showing everything right down to the polka-dots on the characters' underwear. They have been trained to believe that simply *informing* readers about something—a character's anger, say—is a failure of imagination. They believe they must "show" the anger in great detail to make the readers feel it:

> Maxwell's nostrils began to flare, and a wash of red began to rise from his neck upward, into his cheeks and forehead. He narrowed his eyes and his jowls quivered uncontrollably. Little gobs of spit formed at the corners of his mouth. Teeth bared, fists clenched, he spit the words into the public-address system.

This passage is a good example of trying too hard. This is a parody of rage, with nary a body part neglected. Showing and not telling can become a tiresome game: "50 Ways to Express Rage (or sorrow/love/ anxiety/bitterness/despair) Without Once Using the Word." Writers who play this game probably mean well; they believe their descriptive powers can be properly displayed only through one elaborate "show" after another. They become the victims of their own best intentions, for the writing becomes self-conscious and even ridiculous, with passages so loaded with detail that the readers can't find the story. Sometimes it's better to come right out and tell:

> Maxwell felt the full measure of his rage begin to rain down on him.

This description—which is a good example of show-telling (a rage so intense it seems to "rain down")—is terse enough to leave room for other elements of description—dialogue, for example—to complete the picture of Maxwell's anger:

> Maxwell felt the full measure of his rage begin to rain down on him. "You son of a bitch." He spat the words into the public-address system. "First Lester's will, and now this."

In other words, you have to *make decisions* about what to show. How you decide depends on the story. In the preceding example, Maxwell's rage is evidenced by what he says and not how his face looks. In a different story, Maxwell's face might be the better vehicle to "show" his rage.

Choosing What to "Show"

Imagine that your story contains a character named Eulalie, whose age and infirmity drive the storyline. You decide to spend some time "showing" her feebleness:

> Eulalie tottered across the street, her spotted hands curled around the glossy knob of her cane. Through her thin cloth coat you could see the stippled curve of her spine. Before her loomed the oaken doors of the Social Security Administration, stolid and heavy. She sighed. First she'd have to navigate what looked like five thousand granite steps, each of which would require a painful bend of the knee.

In this example, you don't "tell" the readers that Eulalie is old and infirm, and yet her fragility in the face of a hardy world is palpable. Her bent back implies burdens both physical and emotional; the thin coat implies modest means; the building is physically intimidating and promises pain, implying the same about the system it houses. These telling details evoke the readers' empathy, which is what showing is all about. By showing us Eulalie's physical state rather than telling us about it, you make her real, sympathetic, and understandable. This passage works so well because *you are not showing for its own sake*; the description contains important insights into Eulalie's life and character that shore up the story and make it more than a plot.

On the other hand, if you want to focus on Eulalie's considerable strengths *despite* her age, you might want to deliver the information about her age and physical state more directly, and save the "showing" to reveal her personality:

> **Version One:** Eulalie was 92 years old and ailing, but that wasn't going to stop her from marching right down to the Social Security Administration this very afternoon and giving those pink-cheeked little punks a piece of her mind.

In this version, Eulalie's age and infirmity are dispatched with at the outset ("92 years old and ailing"), leaving you free to concentrate on showing what's really important about her. Instead of wasting space "showing" her feebleness, you move instantly to the steel beneath the fragility. She is old enough and crotchety enough to view the clerks as "pink-cheeked little punks"; instead of walking or taking the bus, she plans on "marching right down" to confront them. The readers can imagine the whole story—a little old lady taking on a bureaucracy—from the language contained in that one sentence. And you've established character even further by using language that Eulalie would use, almost as if she were telling the story herself. You are not technically "showing" here; you are informing us that Character A is about to perform Action B. But if the language is rich enough, the story will shimmer whether you're "technically" showing or not. Look at the difference in the passage when you use an objective, expository style:

> **Version Two:** Eulalie, an old woman whose social-security checks had stopped coming since the death of her husband, was

angry. She decided to go to the Social Security Administration building, all the way across town, to find out what happened. She was feisty and crotchety and thought of the buttoned-down clerks as nothing more than pink-cheeked little punks.

The difference between Version One and Version Two is that Eulalie is not present in the second as she is in the first. Version One shows a picture of Eulalie and the possibilities contained in that frail shell. Version Two merely delivers information: Eulalie *is* A and *does* B and *feels* C. It is not showing; it is telling in the most pedantic sense. Again, we're looking at a character on a screen. We cannot enter Eulalie's world in Version Two the way we can in Version One. Instead of hearing echoes of Eulalie's own feisty, crotchety voice, we are *told* that she is feisty and crotchety.

WHEN TO USE NARRATIVE, WHEN TO USE SCENE

As a writer, you get to choose how to manage showing and telling. Jane Austen wrote entire novels in the "telling" style; Philip Roth's novel *Deception* is rendered wholly in dialogue, an extended "show." Reread some favorite stories or novels and identify the passages that tell, the ones that show, and the ones that combine the two. It can be an enlightening and inspiring exercise to see how admired authors handle the balance. Before you try imitating Roth or Austen, however, you should familiarize yourself with the practice of combining scene and narrative.

Generally speaking, when a story calls for some action, you write a scene. But some action is more important than other action. If you are writing a story about a woman who goes to the local butcher to buy some meat and finds the poor man bludgeoned to death behind the counter with his apron wrapped around his neck, you probably will render that action in s[,]ene rather than narrative. However, if the story is really about the woman herself and not the crime she witnessed, you might want to skip that scene altogether. Maybe the story depends more on how she describes the murder to others, over and over again. Witnessing the aftermath of a murder gives her an identity, a status in her family or town that she never dreamed of having.

You title the story "Witness," and begin by "telling":

> On Tuesday Ellen Kornbluth witnessed a murder. Or close enough. She saw the butcher, dead on his stained tile floor, the bloody apron wrapped around his poor pulverized head. Then she saw the orange tail of the murderer's coat, a whisk of movement through the back door.

With two lines of narrative you've introduced the witness and the murder as the *given* of the story; the actual story is revealed a few lines later, at the beginning of this scene:

> "I saw something," she said to her husband. "I saw a murder."
>
> Her husband looked up from his paper. "No, you didn't."
>
> Ellen felt a little flutter of triumph, a cool trilling through her veins. "Oh, but I did. And I've been to the police, and I sat in one of those interview chairs like you see on TV."
>
> He folded the paper once, twice. Set it down on the coffee table that still held the sheen of a special polish Ellen had bought from the hardware store two doors down from the butcher. The dead, murdered butcher. "You saw no such thing," he said, and she could see he was already jealous.
>
> She smoothed her sweater over her bosom, then again down each arm. "I stopped in for the polish, and then I picked up some bread at Mrs. Cutler's, and then I ran into Mrs. Doyle. She had herself a nice pork roast and asked me if I could give her my pineapple pork recipe from memory, which of course I could, and it took about ten, fifteen minutes what with the other things we found to talk about. Ten minutes at least, long enough for a man to do murder." She looked up slyly. "I thought to myself, I'll pick up a nice pork roast myself, since I'm right here in the neighborhood. That's what I thought to myself." She plucked a couple of cat hairs from her cuffs. "The murderer wore an orange coat." She could barely keep from dancing. "I'm the eye witness. That's how the police wrote me down."

Do you see how, in this story, a full-blown murder-discovery scene at the beginning would undercut the essence of the story? Ellen's triumph is not really in witnessing a murder but in being able to puff herself up later as an "eye witness." A scene that shows Ellen walking into town, stopping for furniture polish, stopping for bread, stopping to chat with her friend, entering the butcher shop, calling out for service, walking around the counter, discovering the body, catching sight of the orange coat, calling the police, and so on might be compelling in and of itself, but the story is not set up to support such a scene. That initial action is the not the important action; that's not where the story is. The story begins *after* the discovery of the murder: Ellen's smugness and glee over the butcher's unfortunate demise give the story its tension and drama, and expose the dullness of her life and marriage. The way she smiles slyly and plucks cat hairs off her sweater while trying to keep from dancing is the important action. A scene is entirely called for here: this is the location of the "real" story.

Most experienced writers develop a sixth sense about when a scene is called for to interrupt the narrative. A little voice appears at the back of their consciousness, saying "This is boring," or "The pace is slowing down." The only way to develop this sixth sense is to write a lot (dozens and dozens of stories) and learn by trial and error. In the meantime, though, keep asking yourself *where* the story is, and place your scenes there.

As another example, let's try a story about a wife who has an affair with her husband's boss. Is the dramatic tension of this story contained in the husband-wife relationship, or in the emotional tug-of-war between the wife and the lover? Try the story both ways. You might find that the story interests you most when the husband and wife are having an ostensibly normal dinner at home. The phone rings. She answers. It's the boss (her lover), wanting some information from the husband about an important account. He can't come to the phone because he's in the happy process of feeding their small son, whom he adores, so she relays messages back and forth, having her own illicit conversation with her lover at the same time. Good scene. Great descriptive possibilities, loaded with nuance. This is where a scene belongs, where the real story (the husband-wife relationship) occurs. The wife-lover part of the story, which is less important, can be delivered through narrative—

She saw him twice a week, at the same hotel. For two hours she would pretend to be a character from a movie, charming and irresistible and living a life far from the cereal-stained countertops of their too-small apartment.

A full-blown scene showing the wife-lover liaison and what they say to each other and how they conduct their hello and goodbye would feel like extra weight in the story, a sluggish spot in need of cutting, because the affair is almost irrelevant to the real story.

On the other hand (in fiction there is always another hand), the wife-lover relationship may be the part that interests you most. Suppose the woman meets the lover in the hotel at the usual time, but because she can't find a babysitter she brings the boy along. The lover is miffed; the woman is hurt that after all this time the lover isn't content to "just talk" for a few hours, and also that he doesn't seem interested at all in her adored little boy. The scene could follow their desultory conversation, the arrival of room service (which the rambunctious boy accidentally knocks over) and an argument which the woman comes to realize is their breaking up. On the way home she is surprised to realize that she's looking forward to seeing her husband because of the way his face lights up whenever he sees the boy. In this version of the story, wife-lover is more important than wife-husband: the story is about a woman leaving her lover, not about whom she is leaving him for. The child is the key to the breakup, not the husband. In this case it's the husband-wife part that can be dispatched through narrative:

> Mark was the dependable sort, always on time. He was the one who remembered to send birthday cards to the various members of the family. And he was more mother than she was. He was the one who liked to read bedtime stories and wrap their son's peach-colored body in a thick towel after a bath.

This narrative serves the proper purpose of describing the wife more than the husband. We get a sense of what she *isn't* (maternal, dependable) by reading a description of what he *is*. You don't need a scene to show the father's devotion, because that's not where the story is.

One more story. This one is about a man named Ethan who, deserted six months ago by his wife, is struggling to forge a relationship with his seven-year-old son:

> In July, six months after Jackie had left him and his son to

fend for themselves, Ethan decided to give the boy a party. He was seven, a difficult age, Ethan thought, always whining about something. The party would be something new, a fresh start for both of them. A celebration.

The children arrived in several clusters, according to what street they lived on. Ethan forced his son to stand at the door and hand out a pointy hat to each child that entered the house. The afternoon was a disaster, ending with a couple of bloody noses and a wedge of cake stuffed through the wire bars of the bird cage. One little boy was taken with cramps so severe Ethan began to wonder if he'd paid enough attention to what he'd mixed into the cake. Gamely he'd hosted a round of "Pin the Tail on the Donkey" and then a treasure hunt, only to discover that most seven-year-olds were jaded old men, even the girls, unaffected by the wide-eyed wonder he remembered from his own youth. The giddy celebration of life that Ethan had anticipated had not come to pass, and he sat amongst the wreckage of damp streamers and crazy glue wondering why.

This is a good example of a first draft that shows a writer in search of a story. The narrative is part summary, part imagery, and jams a lot of action—an entire afternoon's worth, in fact—into a very small space. This paragraph could serve as an outline for a fifteen-page story. We have a setup (father giving party to "start fresh"); a conflict (son won't cooperate except by force); a rising action (the events of the party); a climax (the party goes out of control); and a resolution (father left among wreckage). What we don't have, however, are the subtle descriptions that reveal the "real" story, the subtext: How do Ethan's feelings change over the course of the story? What else is happening in Ethan's life that makes the success of the party so important to him? How does he really feel about his son? In other words, we haven't located the story yet.

How do you "find" the story? Begin by slowing down. Take one moment of the narrative that interests you and expand that moment into a scene to see if you can discover what's going on:

Ethan closed his hands over his son's knobby shoulders. "You're going to stand here and pass out hats if I have to hold you here myself."

"I don't want a party," Billy whined. "I don't like those kids." He whipped around, wrenching his shoulders from Ethan's grasp, and gave him that straight-line mouth that reminded him of Jackie before she left them. He was going to be just like her, the glass half empty, always half empty.

"You're just going to have to learn to get along, Billy," Ethan said. He could hear the soft wheedling he had often used with Jackie. "Parties are nice. It's what nice people do. It's part of the social intercourse." He sighed, listening to himself. "It's a good world out there. No one's out to get you." He smiled extravagantly, pointing out the door. "There's Timmy. You like Timmy. Now, aren't you glad we did this?"

Billy frowned deeply, and Ethan could see the word *No* forming on the bow-shaped mouth he'd inherited from his mother. The boy took a breath, and before Ethan knew what he was doing he'd slapped the word from Billy's face with the flat of his hand.

Ironically, the scene gives you far more insight into your characters than did the original narrative, which was packed solid with information. When you compare the boy to the mother early in the scene ("that straight-line mouth"), you discover something: everything that happens between Ethan and Billy will echo the relationship between Ethan and Jackie. Ethan's repressed rage will be acted out on Billy. The original narrative—though full of practical information (length of the separation, Ethan's hope for the party, the individual events of the party)—could never give you these insights. Through scene, you "found" the story.

For describing something wildly disappointing or moving or confounding, a scene almost always does the trick better than narrative. The complexities of human behavior are best described by what the characters themselves say and do, rather than through a narrative interpretation of what they say and do. In the above examples, the difference between

> Ethan forced his son to stand at the door and hand out a pointy hat to each child that entered the house. The afternoon was a disaster. . . .

and

> Ethan closed his hands over his son's knobby shoulders.
> "You're going to stand here and pass out hats if I have to hold
> you here myself."
>   . . . [Billy] whipped around, wrenching his shoulders from
> Ethan's grasp, and gave him that straight-line mouth that re-
> minded him of Jackie before she left them.

is about five shades of meaning. The scene offers an instant reading
of the father-mother-son triangle. If you find yourself confounded by
one human entanglement after another in pages of straight narrative,
stop and ask yourself if a scene would help light your way.

Another time when scene can rescue a story is when you are
working with a character that could be easily labeled a "type." The
following line— "Cindy was a flirt"—can be improved with some
showier telling—"Cindy was a green-eyed blond who could spot a
Yalie from the distance of, say, a dance floor." But it still doesn't do
much but lie on the page. A flirt is a cliché. Green-eyed blonds are the
stuff of TV cop shows. A scene does the trick much more effectively:

> Cindy racketed into the room, wearing her roommate's tiny
> spangled dress. "Eldon," she cooed, offering her one bare
> hand. "Hasn't it been ages?" She slid a finger gingerly along
> the inside of his lapel and smiled.

Of course, this passage isn't long enough to be technically considered
a scene, but it does have scenic properties. It serves a purpose (to
show Cindy's flirtatious character); it contains dialogue; it has a beginning (her entrance), a middle (her dialogue) and an end (her gesture); and it moves the story forward (someone has to react to her
action).

By showing Cindy's flirtatiousness through scene rather than telling the readers that she's a flirt, you are giving her some individuality
and stretching the limitations of stereotype. The sleaze, the goody-
goody, the bitter old man, the blushing bride—all these cardboard
cutouts can be brought to life through scene. An elderly character
described as "a bitter old man" is little more than a cliché. This same
old man shown tearing up his address book or disconnecting his
phone becomes a unique character that breaks stereotype.

WRAP-UP

"Show, don't tell" is merely a guideline for beginning writers, not a rule. A good story can be "told" as well as "shown," and usually a combination of the two techniques yields the most satisfying descriptions. Generally speaking, you show through scene and tell through narrative.

Scenes are most effective when you are trying to reveal the complex interplay between characters, or between a character and himself. Instead of telling the readers that a character is painfully shy, you might shape a scene around that shyness: for instance, somebody could challenge the shy character's religious beliefs while she's minding her own business in the grocery line.

Narrative is most effective when you are trying to fill in background information or move quickly through time to connect two scenes. Instead of writing a full-scale scene in which a young couple worries about how to tell their folks about their recent elopement, you could dispatch the information through a line or two of narrative: "On the way home they decided to tell her parents, who were the soft-spoken ones, and leave his blustering parents in the dark."

Too much scene can make a story seem drawn out, even endless; too much narrative can make a story feel dry and expository. A story takes on so much life—not to mention a pleasing shape—when you move back and forth between scene and narrative. Using the techniques together offers you the most opportunity to vary your descriptions, to give readers an accurate mental picture of the story you wish to tell.

Showing and telling both have a place in good fiction. You may have been taught that "showing" is good and "telling" is bad: if so, rethink your position! With care and attention to language, you can write a beautiful story through showing alone, telling alone, or through a pleasing combination.

CHAPTER 3

DESCRIPTION AND FORWARD MOTION

GOOD STORIES MOVE. They start at the beginning, move through the middle, and end at the end. This is not as simple as it sounds.

Without forward movement, even good characters can find themselves in dull stories. Characters can't just sit around ruminating; they have to do things, say things, go places, interact with people and institutions and their own impulses. A man thinking about death is not a story; a man building his own coffin is. Be wary of stories in which your characters reflect and remember and wonder a lot. Is all that wondering getting them from point A to point B?

Don't ask who your character is; ask what your character does. Trust that she will reveal herself to you through her words and deeds. You might think you know exactly who she is at the outset—she is your creation, after all—but until you take her through at least one draft of the story, until you undertake the burden of describing her in various circumstances, you don't know for certain how she'll react. She may do or say things you didn't plan for; you may have to make alterations in plot (sometimes major ones) to accommodate her emerging personality and motivations. This sense of adventure is what makes writing so much fun.

Good stories are often psychological in nature—character-driven as opposed to plot-driven. Even so, when people ask, "What's the story about?" we tend to describe the plot: A woman loses her child in a store. A man blows up his father's car. A child catches his parents making love. In a very real sense, this physical information is what the story is "about."

What turns plot into story, however, is the *emotional* information that we convey to the readers. (Some writers prefer the word "psychological" to "emotional." I prefer "emotional" because it implies conflicts of the heart as well as the mind.) Emotional information reflects a character's inner landscape: A woman discovers the melancholy of her marriage. A man discovers his hatred for his father. A child discovers his separateness from his parents. These are the same emotional discoveries that make real life so interesting and horrifying and beautiful and compelling. Gather some characters together, give them something to react to, and you've got the ingredients of a story that can move, like life, on two levels: physical and emotional.

HOW STORIES MOVE

Forward movement in fiction is twofold: physical and emotional. *Physical movement* is the movement of the plot from beginning to end:

1. In a department store, mother berates child for swiping several stuffed animals from toy department; now in the hardware department, she "looks away" for a few moments; child disappears.
2. Father makes a scene, begins ordering everyone around; entire store engages in search for child.
3. Mother searches Home section of the store, where beautiful furnishings are arranged in idealized "rooms."
4. Mother finds child asleep on canopy bed in store display, toy animals gathered tightly around her. Mother lies down next to child.

Physical movement, as you can see, follows a plot line. First A happens, then B, then C. When your plot stalls on you, the story stops moving.

The other kind of forward movement, *emotional movement*, follows the development of character rather than plot:

1. Mother's irritation with child stems from a succession of inconsequential fights with her husband. He's with her now because he can't "trust her" to pick out the right kind of

porch light by herself. Mother's inattention occurs when she becomes fascinated with another couple and their child. She contemplates their beauty and peacefulness. When she turns around, her own child is missing.

2. Father's tirade makes mother feel eerily calm. She begins her own search, awed by her composure. She thinks of it as "competence."

3. Mother searches among home furnishings. The beauty and implied family harmony of the displays devastate her. She imagines her husband raging through a different part of the store, and begins to imagine all the ways he will blame her when the child is found. She refuses to imagine a scenario in which the child is not found.

4. Mother finds child in bed display; recognizes her own need for refuge from her husband's harsh judgment. Succumbs to the temptation of the beautiful canopy bed and all the peace and safety it implies.

In this example, plot and character are inextricable: the physical content moves with the emotional. One can exist without the other, but both are enriched by the other's presence. A story that featured this same character standing in a store longing for an idealized family life would not be very interesting; a story that featured only the action of a couple searching a store for their lost child might be interesting but not very rich.

Stories move forward most seamlessly when plot and character mesh. As you move the mother through the physical line (plot) of the story, you can illuminate her emotional progress (character) through her observations. At the beginning, before the child is gone, she observes things somewhat coldly:

> The store was high-ceilinged and bright, punctuated by straight lines: long corridors laid out like streets; grids of steel that held the harsh overhead lights; upright black shelves that housed the switchboxes her husband was pawing through. His own straight lines were turned away from her—his shoulders and back and the grim bottom edge of his hairline.

Notice how this description is all lines and edges; notice also the hardness of the language: *punctuated, harsh, grim, edge.* Later, during

the search for the child, her observations become gentler, even surreal, suggestive of longing:

> She searched through a grouping of stuffed chairs gathered
> like a roomful of uncles after Thanksgiving dinner.

Or:

> She saw a succession of porcelain vases, round and con-
> stant, set on the honeyed tables as if waiting for the flowers
> the husband has just brought home.

Notice how the words change; something is happening inside her.
The same store that a moment ago had "harsh light" is now full
of comfortable chairs and domestic-looking vases. Emotional
movement is contained in subtle descriptions that take the character
through the motion of the plot toward some discovery or revelation
or turning point. A plot is critical, but *which* plot is almost irrelevant. This woman's turning point could have come during a car
crash or a visit to a museum or a bout with illness—any scenario
that could accommodate themes of refuge. The lost child is one of
a thousand possibilities for this particular character's emotional
development.

You don't want your story to move at the same rate from start to
finish. A story's pace is controlled by the physical and emotional
goings-on in the story, and those goings-on are controlled by description. In this story about the lost child, the pace should probably
quicken as the search expands, creating tension (will the child be
found?) that reflects the character's increasing panic. At the beginning of the search, the description could be almost leisurely; after
all, the child is probably right around the corner, or obscured behind
a store display:

> She walked to the end of the aisle, past a brilliantly colored
> pyramid of paint cans. She could imagine the brazen colors
> catching her little girl's interest. Each can resembled the torso
> of a brand-new crayon. She peered around the jagged shape
> and saw nothing but more cans of paint, their chrome handles
> glinting under the light.

Notice the calm, unworried quality of this narrative. The mother is allowing herself time to imagine herself in her child's place, and is herself noticing, if not admiring, little details about the store: the shape of the paint display, the appearance of the cans, the play of light. She is also "walking," not running or lurching, and "peering," not scanning or checking or glancing. In other words, the mother, like the description, is not yet moving very fast.

When the mother does not find the child within the first couple of minutes, though, the stakes suddenly rise. The child could indeed be lost, or worse, abducted. Both the physical and emotional pace of the story are affected. The mother's heart speeds up, and so does the description:

> Aisle six, wrenches. Nothing. She rounded the corner and fled down aisle seven. Screws, wedges, hinges, bolts, nothing. Aisle eight, nine, ten. Nothing but hubcaps and headlights. "Mitzi!" she called, her voice jarring against all that steel and chrome. "Mitzi, answer me, damn it, can you hear me?"

Do you see how you've quickened the pace by using short, staccato sentences? Neither you nor your character can afford to linger over details here. You are giving bare-bones information, for the character is no longer capable of becoming distracted by what she *can* see; she is too preoccupied with what she cannot see: her daughter. The emotional content of the story at this point cannot support a physically slow description.

By the time we approach the end of the story, the search has gone on for a while and erupted into a full-blown family crisis. The father's been yelling at everybody in the store, especially the mother. The mother's initial burst of energy has been dulled by her husband's cruelty and the futility of her search. She is now wandering blindly through the Home section, broken down by fatigue and sadness, not only because of the lost child but because of what she has come to see as a lost chance for a happy family life, whether or not the child is found. Here, you can slow the pace again, for the story is about to end, and the mother is beginning to give up:

> She wandered into a rounded, windowed section of the store that was dressed up to resemble a succession of bedrooms, each more sumptuous than the next. Yards of canopy. Eyelet lace. Sugar-colored pillows she wanted to disappear into. Was

everything white, or was she only imagining it? Had the day's revelations bled the color from her eyes? White, everything white: sheets and towels folded into pearly mounds, doilies and ruffles and washcloths scattered like snowdrifts against cloth-covered tables. And there, sleeping like a pixie on a fresh expanse of cotton, lay her daughter, her white-blond hair dissolving against a lace coverlet.

The mother is so exhausted that her surroundings become surreal, and the frothy description reinforces everything she's experiencing emotionally. The story's physical description has kept perfect pace with its emotional content.

CREATING CONTEXT

Sometimes a story demands more than just a plot to move its emotional content forward. When a story becomes very complicated, or a little too crowded with characters, or stretched over a long period of time, you may want to create a *context*. Context is the descriptive background in a story that sheds light on its meaning. Context is larger than plot; it gives the characters a larger arena in which to hate or love each other, to discover or destroy themselves, to fall under or triumph over adversity.

Contexts can be large: World War II, the Catholic Church, death. Contexts can also be small: winter, a wedding, a hometown. Context provides forward motion at the emotional level, using symbols and metaphors that reinforce emerging themes in a story. It also can serve the practical purpose of organizing the physical movement of a story into beginning, middle, and end. For example, a story told in the context of weather can follow a season or seasons for its beginning, middle, and end: the beginning unfolds during planting, the middle during harvesting, the end during the dormant winter. At the same time, the context reinforces developments in character: a woman's suntanned face gives way to winter-bitten skin that reflects her gathering bitterness.

In Edith Wharton's *Ethan Frome*, the plot follows Ethan's doomed affair of the heart with Mattie Silver, the "companion" of Ethan's sickly and querulous wife. It is a dark story told in the context of the cruel New England winter. After a brief prologue, the story opens this way:

> The village lay under two feet of snow, with drifts at the windy corners. In a sky of iron the points of the Dipper hung like icicles and Orion flashed his cold fires. The moon had set, but the night was so transparent that the white house-fronts between the elms looked gray against the snow, clumps of bushes made black stains on it, and the basement windows of the church sent shafts of yellow light far across the endless undulations.

This descriptive passage sets up a context that will be carried through the novel—the characters cannot escape the literal and metaphorical cold. And yet the shafts of yellow light sent undulating over the snow deliver a hint that warmth is possible even in this unforgiving place. The love that develops between Ethan and Mattie is that drop of warmth, but the landscape literally and figuratively becomes their doom. As the story progresses, Wharton softens the landscape a bit when Ethan begins to imagine himself and Mattie together:

> They finished supper, and while Mattie cleared the table Ethan went to look at the cows and then took a last turn about the house. The earth lay dark under a muffled sky and the air was so still that now and then he heard a lump of snow come thumping down from a tree far off on the edge of the wood-lot.

Even though the landscape is softened here—the domestic quiet implied by the cows and the muffled sky—Wharton preserves an unrelenting sense of foreboding with that disquieting, far-off thumping of snow. The context remains steady throughout, with repeated images of sterility and starkness and frozen ground, as the physical and emotional lines of the story culminate in a toboggan accident that destroys Mattie and Ethan in different ways.

The plot of Jane Smiley's novel *A Thousand Acres* unfolds in the huge context of land—the family-owned, generations-old "thousand acres" of the title. The land is something that must be reckoned with at every turn in the book, for the land is the characters' livelihood and also their prison. It is both beautiful and menacing. The context provides an irony that resonates throughout this story of a multitude of family betrayals set into motion by the patriarch's dividing of the land. (It's a retelling of *King Lear*.) Because the land must be tended to in all its seasons, the context provides a blueprint for moving the plot along. Ginny, the narrator, begins and ends her story by describing the land:

> ... you could see our buildings, a mile distant, at the southern edge of the farm. A mile to the east, you could see three silos that marked the northeastern corner, and if you raked your gaze from the silos to the house and barn, then back again, you would take in the immensity of the piece of land my father owned, six hundred forty acres, a whole section, paid for, no encumbrances, as flat and fertile, black, friable, and exposed as any piece of land on the face of the earth. ...
>
> ... I thought it appropriate and desirable that the great circle of the flat earth spreading out from the T intersection of County Road 686 and Cabot Street Road be ours. A thousand acres. It was that simple.

The ensuing story is anything but simple, and ends with another view of the same land:

> Let us say that each vanished person left me something, and that I feel my inheritance when I am reminded of one of them. When I am reminded of Jess, I think of the loop of poison we drank from, the water running down through the soil, into the drainage wells, into the lightless mysterious underground chemical sea, then being drawn up, cold and appetizing, from the drinking well into Rose's faucet, my faucet. I am reminded of Jess when I drive in the country, and see the anhydrous trucks in the distance, or the herbicide incorporators, or the farmers plowing their fields in the fall, or hills that are ringed with black earth and crowned with soil so pale that the corn only stands in it, as in gravel, because there are no nutrients to draw from it.

The poison beneath the land echoes the poison beneath the family relationships. The context of land reinforces every lie and betrayal the characters inflict on one another.

Not all contexts are this large. The breadth of the story should dictate the breadth of the context. A story about a marriage breaking up would work quite well in a small context: the story takes place over the course of an exceptionally dry summer, say, its attendant images of burnt lawns and dead flowers reinforcing the story's emotional content. A story about the dissolution of an entire family might work well in a larger context such as a five-year drought or a civil war.

Let's start small, with a story about a middle-aged woman named Harriet who comes to realize that she has squandered her life. That's the "story," the emotional content; the plot, however, takes her through the machinations of her first dinner party in twenty years. Her model for this party is a wine ad she saw in a magazine. The ad depicts a genteel, dress-up dinner party—an image so vivid in Harriet's mind that it becomes the context for the story. This context contains symbols of an elegant, upper-crust lifestyle which contrasts nicely with Harriet's middle-class limitations. It also has the potential for illuminating themes like falseness and self-deception. Also, the dinner party gives you a blueprint for moving the plot forward: appetizers, main course, dessert.

Suppose you begin the story by showing Harriet getting the appetizers ready in the kitchen. As in all the previous examples, careful description heightens context and connects the story's physical and emotional forward movement:

> She put one bright canapé after another onto a silver tray, fretting over each rose-shaped radish, each olive-topped cream-cheese cracker, each polished cherry, each frilly spray of parsley. She frowned. The props that had suggested whimsy in the magazine photograph took on an air of desperate excess when crowded onto her grandmother's silver platter. She tried to imagine the wine-blushed faces in that ad, all of them frantically happy. What, exactly, were they looking at? The food? Each other? Their own fabulousness? Harriet sighed. It was too late now. The menu was set, the table decorated, the guests invited and arrived. Whatever she had overlooked would have to wait.

By describing the tray of hors d'oeuvres so vividly and then revealing Harriet's disappointment, you imply that this is more than just a dinner party to Harriet, and that she's beginning to suspect that her lavish expectations may not be met. The context begins to form, for what reader has not longed to step into the midst of an ad like the one Harriet is remembering? Because you render Harriet's reaction to the ad in such precise detail ("wine-blushed," "frantically happy"), your readers have no choice but to measure Harriet's party against the wine-ad party.

What's next? Suppose Harriet glances out the kitchen door and spots her husband, Marty, looking stiff and unyielding among the drift of guests, whom she realizes are all *her* friends:

> She let the door fall closed, picked up her burgeoning tray and practiced moving with it in the clean privacy of her kitchen. She stopped, listening once again to the light-hearted weave of voices, and suddenly remembered certain old friends—all those laughing girls!—who had gone off to work or traveled out of state or otherwise drifted away.
>
> "Hors d'oeuvres," she called cheerily, brandishing her tray. Everyone looked up. The women were dressed in skirts and pantsuits, the men in ordinary shirts, as though they had arrived here straight from the office.

In this passage, you move the story forward emotionally, and that emotional movement is made richer by the context. Notice how even small contextual details reveal character: Harriet's "burgeoning tray" harkens back to the wine-ad party in all its bounty, but the phrase also reminds us of Harriet's burgeoning expectations, and her dim sense of her own "desperate excess." Because we recognize that Harriet's hope is for the wine-ad party, we understand without being told that Harriet is disappointed to see the "skirts and pantsuits" and "ordinary shirts."

In the next scene, Harriet circulates through her living room with the tray, realizing that she doesn't actually know any of her guests very well. She makes little stabs at small talk, remembering her earlier expectations:

> She had imagined herself glancing around gaily, discussing things topical and stimulating. She had imagined glasses raised in convivial gladness. How extravagant the women's dresses, how smooth and muscular their exposed shoulders. And the men! Leaning forward, listening to her opinions, relaxed and genial, stretching in their beautiful silk shirts.

Even though Harriet is remembering past thoughts in a brief flashback, the emotional content of the story is moving forward because you are revealing even more about Harriet's self-delusion. The passage is full of Harriet's foolishness—convivial gladness and beautiful silk shirts, indeed!—almost as if she is remembering the wine ad as something she actually experienced. The wine-ad image of "... men leaning forward, listening to her opinions, relaxed and genial ..." suggests this lonely woman's desperate hope for something that will never happen.

Using the context as a story organizer, you can enter the story's middle through the vehicle of a main course. The action accelerates and the stakes rise. Harriet tries vainly to strike up some "topical" conversation with the increasingly taciturn guests; Marty picks a fight with the man sitting across from him; Harriet takes the man's side, which triggers another argument between her and Marty; finally, the guests one by one remember other appointments or babysitters at home and drift off.

The end of the story is signalled by the end of the party. Marty stalks upstairs without a word, leaving Harriet alone to preside over the half-eaten remains of her elaborate dinner:

> Harriet drew herself up and collected the dirty plates and took them to the kitchen. She could see traces of the delicate pattern—little blue flowers—between gobs of sauce and bits of meat and the frayed heads of asparagus. Marty was moving through their bedroom overhead, his steps heavy and grave. Along the counter twelve cuts of cheesecake were lined up on filigreed dessert plates, one perfect cherry atop each slice. She looked closer: the cherries had begun to bleed, leaving uneven drizzles along the lovely white wedges. Harriet shook her head, clucking to herself. She had left them out too long. She had not paid enough attention. Not that it mattered; there was nobody here to eat them.

Notice how the physical and emotional endings coincide. Harriet rues her bleeding cheesecakes, and the nature of that observation (the marred appearance of the white cake) gives your readers to understand what Harriet now realizes: Not only has the party been a dismal failure, but so has her life. She has left *herself* "out [of life] too long," and is only now feeling the enormity of her exile.

Ethan Frome draws its power from the similarity between the story and its context—the hopeless people and the hopeless weather. This little story about Harriet draws its power from the *contrast* between the story and its context—the real party and the wine-ad party. Context can work with or against a story with equally satisfying results.

FORWARD MOTION AND PHYSICAL DESCRIPTION

There is no greater (nor annoying) motion-stopper than immobile chunks of physical description. A head-to-toe tour of a character's appearance, clothing, etc., before we know anything else about him, is at best ineffective and at worst counterproductive. Not only is this technique clunky and amateurish, it stops the natural flow of the story. The inexperienced writer often introduces characters this way:

> At the knock on the door, Alan looked up from his desk. Walter Clayton ambled across the carpet, holding out one hand. "I've been looking forward," he said.
> Walter Clayton was thirty-five years old, dark-haired, with blue eyes that looked forced open. He liked basketball, but at five-feet-two wasn't tall enough to play. His feet were small and square. His graying hair was parted severely to one side and his ears were pinned close to his head. The only thing big about him was his hands: large and meaty, with thick, calloused fingers and curiously shellacked nails. He wore a suit of blended silk, and his cuffs protruded an elegant half-inch below the sleeves. As he sat down his pant legs rode up, revealing an extraordinary pair of chartreuse wool socks.

This is not bad description; in fact, it is good description. The details are precise and interesting. The problem is that the descriptive information is given all at once. We are left to drum our fingers until the writer gets back to the plot. I recently read a good novel, a well-written psychological thriller, in which *every single character* was introduced this way. It became distracting, then mildly amusing ("I wonder if he knows he's doing this?"), and finally infuriating. You don't want to tamper this way with your readers' good graces.

Lack of movement is not the only problem with this kind of "chunk" description. As I discovered from reading the aforementioned novel, when readers are introduced to a character in this way, they will not remember what the character looks like later on. Despite your heroic efforts at description, readers tend to accept chunks of physical description as "snapshots" that they look at once and then forget. The characters get short shrift! Descriptions should guide readers to the most telling, characterizing details; when all the details are lumped together they take on equal weight. Reading a long, detailed physical description is like looking at a painting from a distance of two inches: it becomes a big blob that's hard to keep in perspective. Deliver physical characteristics a few at a time, and the character in question becomes much more seeable:

> At the knock on the door, Alan looked up from his desk. Walter Clayton ambled across the carpet, holding out one meaty hand. "I've been looking forward," he said.
> Alan shook Walter's hand. "Have a seat."
> As Walter Clayton sat, the cuff of his immaculate silk pants rode up to reveal a pair of chartreuse socks. "Abby sent me," he said. "But of course you know that."
> Alan stared at the small round face, the blue eyes that looked forced open. "You have information for me, Mr. Clayton?" he said, glancing down at the preposterous socks.
> "I do," Walter Clayton said. He patted the sides of his graying hair. "Yes, indeed." He gave out a thin-lipped grin. "Oh, I do, indeed."

Do you see how this one-detail-at-a-time description turns Walter Clayton from a mannequin in a storefront to a full-blooded character? We discover the eccentric details of Walter's physical appearance at the same time he is being revealed as a character, and therefore each detail takes on added significance. The details *mean* something. If details emerge one by one in increasing significance, the character encroaches on our consciousness in a way that makes him real, and the story rolls along without missing a beat.

FLASHBACKS AND THEIR PROBLEMS

Used judiciously, the flashback is a magnificent descriptive tool. Flashbacks move a story back in time, giving us insights about characters we don't know well.

Imagine you're writing a story about Marcus, a ruthless inside trader who seems to have no conscience. Your descriptions are as deliberately dispassionate as his life: he goes to work early in the morning, when the sky is a "low, steely ceiling"; his office is "fluorescent and silent," and his apartment is furnished with "chrome and leather, with a high-tech kitchen as clean as a space station." After Marcus tells his fiancee that her clothes aren't right for the party he wants to take her to, you insert a brief flashback that shows Marcus as a boy on a dirt-poor Iowa farm, putting on a handed-down suit for his father's funeral.

The descriptions in the flashback, which suggest humiliation and despair, contrast with the hard, unemotional imagery of the present-time story. Paradoxically, flashbacks can move stories backward and forward at the same time. This story takes a leap forward as we gain a fuller understanding of Marcus. We can suddenly see why he is ashamed of his fiancee's clothing and why he might want to live the way he does. Flashbacks can flesh out your characters, add to the readers' perceptions, and change the mood or direction of a story.

Flashbacks are not always brief, nor do they always move stories forward. This is not to say that long flashbacks are bad. They can be badly handled, however, and often are. They may feature awkward transitions; they may take too long; they may contain flashbacks within flashbacks; they may deliver chunks of information that stop the action and therefore have a dry, expository quality. All of these drawbacks affect the natural movement that good stories require.

Used effectively, flashbacks enhance the emotional movement of a story, deepen the story's imagery (an image that figures prominently in a flashback takes on extra meaning when used again in the main body of the story), and organize a story by weaving information into the narrative at critical times. Most important, they can enhance the descriptive nature of a story by shoring up some of the more elusive aspects of a character. Like scenes (many flashbacks *are* scenes, in fact), flashbacks can help you locate your story. That Iowa farm may be the key to understanding Marcus's present motives; the story's heart is not on Wall Street but back in Iowa.

Even well-written flashbacks pose risks. One, readers may become impatient to return to the present action; two, they may become so engrossed in the flashback that they're disappointed to get back to the present action; three, they may feel they've been absented so long from the present action that they can't very easily pick up the thread of the original story. My own rule of thumb about flashbacks is that they are such a bother and so hard to make seamless that they should be used only when you have no other workable descriptive choices.

Transitions

The most common problem with flashbacks is getting into and out of them. When introducing flashbacks, inexperienced writers often resort to devices like the following:

> I opened the drawer to my mother's desk and discovered the emerald ring. The sight of it brought me back to that day nearly thirty years ago when she gathered us into the living room to tell us she was leaving.
> "Boys," she said. "Come here. Mama has something to tell you."

Or:

> Roland slipped the letter through the gold-painted mail slot and paused. Something about the deeply cut design of the door reminded him of another door, another life, another time . . .
> It was 1955 when he had first gone to the lumberyard to get some wood for a new door. His father took him down in the truck, and he loved the rough sounds that rattled up through the seat as they moved over the pocked road.

These transitions are burdensome and somewhat awkward, and take away from the nice flashbacks that they introduce. Never use ellipses (. . .) to telegraph a passage back in time. It looks amateurish and usually makes your opening line seem like a voice-over in a B movie. Also, avoid phrases like "it brought me back to" or "suddenly I remembered." Forget the fanfare and enter the flashback directly:

> I opened the drawer to my mother's desk and discovered the emerald ring she had been wearing the night she told us

she was leaving. I was six. "Boys," she said. "Come here. Mama has something to tell you."

Or:

> Roland slipped the letter through the gold-painted mail slot and paused. The deep cut of the door was similar to the one he and his father had once designed for the house in Cutler. His father had driven him down to the lumber yard in Grandad's 1955 Chevy pickup, and he loved the rough sounds that rattled up through the seat as they moved over the pocked road.

Do you see the difference? Here, you enter the flashback with no "I remember" prologue of any kind. The transition in time barely makes a ripple in the story's forward motion.

Coming back out of flashbacks can be tricky as well. The shorter the flashback, the easier the return:

> Holly turned the key and held her breath. Last week at this time it had been Alfred on the other side of the door, lounging in her favorite chair, drinking her good sherry, his fingers coiling around the stem of the glass as he smiled up at her. "Hello, Sweetheart," he said, his upper lip curling. Maybe she should have given him the money. She pushed open the door, half expecting to see him again, but the only living creature was the cat slumbering on the sofa.

The character's transition from remembering last-week Alfred to pushing open today's door is seamless, because you haven't diverted the readers from the present action long enough for them to forget anything. Only three sentences of flashback intrude on the present-time story.

Transition problems usually crop up when you try to return to the main story after a flashback of several paragraphs, or several pages, or, in some cases, several chapters. In case the readers have forgotten the present-time story, you announce its return with a drum roll:

> . . . She waved goodbye to the birds that eddied above the sea-green fields of her grandmother's saltwater farm.
>
> The sound of bells brought her back to the present.

Or:

> . . . The sight of his wife's fingers moving over the piano's shiny keys would forever remain a memory he kept to himself.
> But that was all in the past; Mr. Goldberg rubbed his eyes and turned again to his papers, which suddenly looked thin and pale.

In these returns, you might as well be holding up a cue card: AND NOW, BACK TO OUR STORY IN PROGRESS. To avoid this awkwardness when moving out of flashbacks, use the same direct approach that you would in moving *into* a flashback:

> . . . She waved goodbye to the birds that eddied over the sea-green fields of her grandmother's saltwater farm.
> Bells sounded outside her window. She rose from her desk to look down at the street.

Or:

> . . . The sight of his wife's fingers moving over the piano's shiny keys would forever remain a memory he kept to himself.
> Mr. Goldberg rubbed his eyes. The papers spread on his desk looked thin and pale.

Easy in, easy out. Delete phrases like "brought her back to the present" or "that was in the past" or "suddenly he realized he'd been daydreaming." They are almost never necessary. With longer flashbacks you may want to use asterisks or white space—that is, several blank lines on the page—to signify a major leap from past to present:

> . . . defeated and bereft, Mark staggered over the sidewalk. He wanted only to be alone. He stood in the shelter of a urine-soaked doorway, clutching the gritty lapel of his cousin's jacket.
>
> * * * *
>
> The clock tower struck four as Mark stepped out of the arched doorway of the bank lobby. He stood on the street, squinting up at the sky, hands thrust deep into his pockets.

These physical cues give readers a moment to get their bearings and prepare to re-enter the present-time part of the story. White space in a short story is similar to a chapter break in a novel. It is the author's polite way of telling readers that the scene is changing.

The more unassuming your transitions in and out of flashbacks, the less your story will have an "assembled" quality: *this* part (e.g., the flashback to the Vietnam War) goes here, and *that* part (e.g., the therapy session in 1995) goes there. Assembly is the opposite of flow. To maintain a sense of forward motion and descriptive cohesiveness, make your transitions in and out of flashbacks as invisible as possible. You want your story to feel like an inevitable whole, not a collection of parts.

"Frame" Stories

For some reason inexperienced writers have a penchant for "frame" stories, in which the present-day action frames an extended flashback. For example, the story may open with a man's description of his mother's burial, which triggers in him an extended flashback of the summer his dog died, and how his mother's practical strength helped him accept the death of his beloved pet. Then the story returns to the present-day gravesite where the man is saying his final goodbye to Mom, and the readers are now supposed to have a deeper understanding of his grief. This structure stops motions cold, for the readers spend the bulk of the story wondering when he's going to get back to present action, and what on earth the present action has to do with the extended flashback. The result is just as awful as you'd suspect. Stories like this begin this way:

> I walked the long dirt path to the open gravesite under a white, curiously cold sun. Friends and colleagues murmured their condolences; their voices blended into a quiet, indecipherable stirring in the air. My wife leaned her cheek against my arm as we listened to the minister's bland intonations. When finally they lowered my mother's coffin into the ground, the strong scent of earth brought me back to one unforgettable summer over twenty years ago.
>
> Sparky, our family dog, turned nineteen that summer, a day after I turned nine. My mother thought it would be fun to have a birthday party to which we invited both boys and dogs.

After this awkward introduction to the flashback, the narrator goes on to describe that fateful summer. On the last page he returns to the present in another awkward transition:

> I buried Sparky at the back of my mother's garden with a spade she kept in her tool shed. I stayed there, sitting on the upturned grass, until she came down long after supper to help me pick some flowers to lay on his grave.
>
> Now, twenty years later, as I toss some flowers from that same garden on her grave, I can thank my mother for all she taught me about remembering the dead.

Frame stories almost always have transition problems, because the frame, unbeknownst to the author, is usually unnecessary. The extended flashback usually can stand as a story all by itself. Notice also that the frame makes the story's other problems—principally the sentimental descriptions—much more glaring than they should be. Framing a flashback points a thousand red arrows at it. The most innocent description sags under the burden of momentousness. ("A cherry-red barn?" we ask. "Cherries must be really significant!") Don't do this to yourself. Unless the flashback and the frame are critically, unequivocally interdependent and *there is no other way to merge the past and present*, the frame is irrelevant. A frame like the one in the above example begs the questions: Why not make the flashback the story? Isn't the story about that transforming summer, not about the mother's funeral? Whether or not the mother dies twenty years later, isn't the lesson she taught him during that summer the point of the story? The line that comes after the introduction to the flashback would, with minor adjusting, make a great opening for a story all by itself:

> The summer I turned nine, my dog turned nineteen. My mother gave us both a party.

Bingo, you're moving again! You have dropped the readers into the midst of a story, one that has wonderful descriptive potential. Gone is the clumsy introduction, not to mention the wet blanket of sentimentality that dear old Mom's burial provides. Without the lead-in, the flashback no longer has to support a present-day story that isn't really a story. Instead, the flashback stands alone as a memoir-style narrative told by a reminiscent narrator. No introduction or grand finale required.

In rare cases, a frame *is* necessary. You probably should keep the frame *if the frame part of the story is the direct result of the flashback*: A man is hiding his true identity from his wife and kids, because he's a fugitive from a 20-year-old crime. Also, you should keep the frame *if the frame is more important than the flashback*: A woman's children ask her to tell about the baby she lost fifteen years ago; in the telling, they all realize that the lost baby is the only one the mother ever loved. If you must keep the frame, then avoid pitfalls by relying on the transition rules: easy in, easy out. Use white space if you have to. Don't belabor the "that was then and this is now" point. If you're writing a very long story, or a novel, transitions back and forth are often necessary and can be elegant and subtle as long as you don't introduce them with a drum roll.

Expository Flashbacks

When you have a lot of background information to account for, flashbacks are enticing. In the interest of expediency, you might be tempted to bunch all the background information together like this:

Kit flung open the door. "Betty!" she cried, enfolding the bony form of her only cousin.

"Wait." Betty stiffened. "I have something to tell you first."

Kit looked at her cousin, whom she hadn't seen in years. They had been each other's best friend back on the farm in Montana, young girls who had sat night after night on their grandfather's porch counting fireflies and following the magnificent arcing path of the bats that lived across the road in their uncle Cyrus's barn. Their childhood had been one of loss and redemption. They lost their parents in the same spectacular crash on the Monson Road that people still talked of twenty years later. Earlier that summer they had been shuttled off to their grandmother's farm in Shapleigh where their uncles had identical farms all the way up and down the River Road. Their fathers, the youngest of the eight Harding brothers, were deep into some business deal that required travel and, it seemed, the corralling company of their wives. The girls didn't mind; they loved their uncles, each other, and that string of verdant farms. It was there they had found solace from their grief, in the blond fields of wheat and the borders of stooped trees and the magical, female comfort of each other.

"The farm burned down," Betty said.

Informational flashbacks like this knock a story flat. You open a door to the readers (literally, in this case), then shut it while you fill in the background. In the meantime, we're itching to find out what Betty wants to tell Kit. Their shared childhood may be critical to the story, but it does not have to be described at this particular time, nor all at once. Blocks of information tend to be short on specifics, anyway; the descriptive details start to fall away and get replaced by dull exposition. You'll notice that the above flashback, though it contains a few nice phrases and some pretty images, delivers information that feels irrelevant, at least at this point in the story. Who cares, *right now*, that their parents died? What difference do Uncle Cyrus's bats make, *right now*, when we haven't even heard Betty speak? Background details are best given in the present flow of the story, on a need-to-know basis. Give your description a chance to breathe, instead of choking it into one thick chunk. Move your story forward by dispensing description little by little in a series of brief, delicate flashbacks:

"What do you mean, the farm burned down?" Kit asked. She sat on the plump sofa, pulling Betty down next to her. "You don't mean Grandma's farm."

"I'm sorry," Betty murmured. "There's nothing left. The barn, the outbuildings, the house, nothing. Burned." She looked at Kit. "Nothing to show but a couple of charred porch rails."

Kit put a hand to her mouth, stunned by an image of that beautiful old porch. She and Betty had spent hours there, especially at night, watching the bats dip over the road that separated their grandmother's farm from their uncle's. The night their parents died they had sat all night in the sloped shelter of its roof, their thin arms twined together, watching the empty road.

"I don't believe it," Kit said, shaking her head. "How can a place so beautiful be gone?"

You can continue to fill in details like this as the story progresses. Then, when you must stop to flash back, the flashback becomes a forward-moving narrative in itself, one that concentrates on the important things because the chaff has been weeded out:

> "Sometimes I think God hates us," Betty said. "Seems like heartache has followed us all our lives."
> Kit nodded. The night their parents died had been hot and starless. The two girls had spent the entire day in Uncle Arden's barn, petting the horses, making little forts out of hay. When they made their way back to the house it was long past supper and no one had thought to call them. From far down the road she could hear the frantic blue whine of the sheriff's siren. The driveway was jammed with uncles' cars, every light in the house was blazing, and someone was shouting into the kitchen phone.

This flashback, which could easily go on to describe the rest of the night's events, works well because it comes at a point in the story where the readers are willing to stop a moment to delve into the characters. We have already met Kit and Betty and gotten several hints about their closeness and shared experience through snippets of flashback. Because you've planted the relevant details, we are now ready for the full story. The flashback provides that full story in the nicest sense of the word: it is a *story*, with a beginning, middle, and end, containing its own forward motion.

The Past Perfect

A cautionary note on the use of flashbacks: Beware the past perfect! The past perfect can get you into a flashback, but sometimes you can't find your way out. In the following flashback, the past perfect is in italics:

> He *had been* a good worker in those days. He *had had* his own truck and a crew of two. Every morning he *had gone* down to the post office and waited around for the first stirrings of village life, and by nine o'clock he *had always had* a job. He *had gone* home every night with money in his pocket . . .

Well, you get the idea. For some reason inexperienced writers slip into a deer-in-headlights relationship with the past perfect when writing flashbacks. Once they latch on, they can't move away. But the continued use of "he had done" and "he had said" serves only to remind readers again and again that this is a flashback and not the real story, which makes the movement of the story sluggish and uninteresting.

Don't be afraid to move out of the past perfect quickly, even immediately. In the following example, the simple past tense provides the flashback with a forward movement of its own. (The introductory past-perfect verb is in italics.)

> He *had been* a good worker in those days. He had his own truck and a crew of two. Every morning he went down to the post office and waited around for the first stirrings of village life, and by nine o'clock he had a job. He went home every night with money in his pocket . . .

In most flashbacks the past perfect is required only briefly—for the first one or two verbs—to establish a movement back in time. After that, let the simple past tense pull the flashback forward, especially in flashbacks with a lot of dialogue—nothing is more distracting than "he had said" and "she had answered."

FLASH-FORWARDS

The flash-forward, a little-used fiction technique, gives your readers a glimpse of the future:

> Alison wanders through her new house, wondering how she will possibly fill it. Her sofa and coffee table look like doll furniture under the cavernous ceilings. Even the light switches look foolishly small against the broad white expanses of wall. Twenty years from now, missing the husband and children she does not yet know she will have, she will wander through this same house wondering how she will possibly empty it.

A flash-forward hurtles your readers ahead in the story, sometimes too fast. Flash-forwards can add poignancy and weight to a character's situation, but if you have no compelling reason to telegraph future events you risk being (rightfully) accused of gimmickry. In the preceding example, Alison is a character who is always looking on the other side of the fence, so the brief description of her future is probably appropriate.

Ironically, flash-forwards do not have to be rendered exclusively in future tense. In my novel, *Secret Language*, I use one flash-forward, during the present-tense wedding of Faith, the main character. Faith is remote and wary, terrified of life's ordinary joys. At her wedding, she "steps out of her body" to watch from a safe distance:

> . . . Heat bears down on her from all sides but she cannot warm herself. She's gone cold with the fear of love and the knowledge of her unbelonging, so cold she can barely stand, and so she removes herself from this joyful gathering, steps away from them all while her chilled body stays.
>
> She watches Joe slip the ring over her knuckle. She watches herself murmur "I do," all the faces tensing forward because they cannot hear her.
>
> She will remember this moment many, many times. Remembering, she will believe that if she had only been able to warm herself, if she had only stayed inside her body as she pledged forever and true, she might have learned to live with a man like Joe, a man who loved her.

The movement of tense in this passage is deliberate. First, I move from present tense to the future tense of the flash-forward ("She will remember this moment . . ."). Then the flash-forward itself becomes a passage in which a mini-flashback takes place ("if she had only been able to warm herself. . . ."). This is tricky; I am telegraphing, through flash-forward, a scene in which Faith will look back. Why did I complicate the passage like this? Because the novel is about Faith's journey toward an emotional place where she can finally "warm herself" and indeed "learn to love a man like Joe." Faith is a woman who refuses to live in either the past or the future, only the present, and to place her in both the past and future in this passage serves as a pivot point in the novel. It was the best device I could think of to describe this paradoxical, elusive character. At this point, where flash-forward and flashback converge, the book takes a sudden emotional leap forward.

In our story about Sparky the dog, the flashback became the story because the frame (the mother's funeral) was less important or interesting than the flashback. If you insisted on using the mother's eventual death as a way of adding weight to the story of the boy's ninth summer, a flash-forward would do nicely:

By morning the dog was dead. He was lighter than I expected, his fur still smooth. I followed my mother to the section of our land that looked down over Blue Creek. Tearless and solemn, we buried Sparky next to a growth of mustard flower. My mother let me fill the hole and mound the iron-red earth. The spade was one she sheltered at the back of the toolshed, for it was little-used and almost beautiful: sharp and solid, with a thick handle fashioned out of a light, burled wood; the very spade I would use ten years later at an occasion no less solemn but marked by many tears.

Flashbacks and flash-forwards are satisfying descriptive devices, but beware of using them unless you can articulate your reasons. "To fill in information" is not good enough. You can fill in information a little at a time during the natural forward course of the story. Ask yourself every time: Why am I flashing back? To endear the readers to a not-yet-met character? Fine. To contrast a character's present husband with the former husband? Sure. To create a context that will resonate in a reader's mind as the story progresses? Sounds good. You can probably name a dozen good reasons for using flashback, but if you can accomplish your goal without one, why not save yourself the aggravation?

A WORD ON THE SET PIECE

A set piece is a detour in the path your story takes. It is a fixed descriptive diversion executed with great care: an elaborate description of a horse farm, for example, or a brick-by-brick account of the building of a museum.

Digressions are fun. You're writing about a character in a terrible emotional crisis, and all of a sudden the circus comes to town and you find yourself devoting four and a half pages to the elephant act. Such a set piece can be brilliant and beautiful and a pleasure to read, even if it appears to have only a marginal connection with the rest of the story. If you're going to stop the story's present action, then stop it big! Like a well-crafted flashback, the set piece can take on its own momentum.

A good set piece only *seems* irrelevant to the story at hand. A two-page description of the way rain moves across the prairies may seem like a mere literary detour, but in fact it telegraphs the swift changes that are about to befall the character in the story. A set piece about the building of a skyscraper may be entirely appropriate in a story about a woman building a medical practice, or a parent building a relationship with a difficult child. Also, a set piece may suggest how a character thinks, what a character's moral limits are, and so on. In a story about a retired nurse longing for a more interesting life, the set piece about the circus might highlight the fanfare and theater of the trapeze act. In a story about an ex-con, the same set piece might address the cruelty of forcing animals into cages.

If you find yourself caught up in a set piece, make it count. The description should be delectable, with lots of little-known facts and details that will dazzle your readers. A tour of your grandmother's living room (unless she lives in an igloo or a culvert) probably wouldn't make much of a set piece, but a description of wine-making in Napa Valley might. Readers aren't too cranky about diversions as long as they learn something in the process—something delivered with a descriptive flair, that is.

Finally, be sure the story—or novella, or novel—can support the weight of the digression. A ten-page story can't support a four-page set piece. A ninety-page novella can. A novel, of course, is the roomiest place to peer down those roads not taken.

WRAP-UP

A good story depends on forward motion, and forward motion depends on many aspects of description technique. Stories move on two levels, physical and emotional; when delivering details, you must attend to the emotional as well as the physical content of the story. A character's view of a snowstorm may be lean or sumptuous, depending on his state of mind. Sometimes you have to create a wider descriptive framework—a *context*—in order to handle the emotional complexity of certain stories. A story about a recently widowed man may need the context of a crime-ravaged neighborhood to adequately deliver the sense of caprice and futility that often accompany loss.

The head-to-toe physical description of a character, although a wonderful test of your descriptive powers, can stop a story cold if rendered in large chunks. Try delivering physical details one or two at a time, allowing your readers to get to know a character within the natural forward flow of the story. The characters will be more memorable that way, and you won't have to test your readers' patience by stopping the story every time you want to introduce somebody.

The flashback is another descriptive device that helps your readers get to know a character. Paradoxically, a flashback can move a story forward even though it literally moves backward. As long as the information in the flashback is relevant and interesting—containing the kind of description that engages a reader and illuminates a character—the story will gain momentum. To give flashbacks the best chance of working without stopping forward motion, you must watch for familiar pitfalls. Transitions in and out of flashbacks should be direct and seamless; the flashback should be *part* of a present-action story, and not vice-versa (if the flashback begins to take over the story, then it probably *is* the story); the flashback should contain its own descriptive flow and not be used as a repository for background information; and the past-perfect tense should be replaced by the simple past tense as soon as possible in a flashback (the past perfect serves only to remind readers that the flashback is a diversion from the "real" story).

The flash-forward, on the other hand, is a literal movement forward—a description that announces a future event. Use it sparingly or not at all, for the direct telegraphing of events ruins a story's tension much more often than it adds weight or poignancy.

The set piece is another motion-stopper that can test even the most forgiving reader's good nature. The set piece is a descriptive detour that usually comes from the author's fascination with a subject: how an airplane works; what Monet's gardens at Giverny look like in winter; the history of the Micmac Indians in northern Maine. A successful set piece contains illuminative description and enchanting information. Even if it has only a marginal relationship to the other events of the story, the set piece should suggest something about the way a character thinks or how the events in the story are about to unfold. The story or novel in which the set piece resides must be long enough to contain it; a five-page set piece will burden a short story and brighten a novel.

If forward movement is a problem you struggle with in your fiction, analyze your description techniques. Check for blocky, inert descriptive passages. Check your transitions back and forth in time. Make sure the details enhance both the physical and emotional content. Description is so much more than reportage; it is invention, imagination, and re-creation.

CHAPTER 4

DESCRIPTION AND DIALOGUE

DESCRIPTION AND DIALOGUE are usually discussed as entirely separate techniques. In practice, however, description and dialogue often become inextricable and always have similar functions: to enrich the readers' understanding of a story, to move the story forward, and to help the readers "see" a character. Good dialogue *is* good description.

When a character proclaims, "I'm fed up with you, Arnold. I'm clearing out of here right now," her anger is just as evident as it would be if described through narrative. On the other hand, a long and pointless dialogue sequence in which two characters drink coffee and chat aimlessly about dog grooming stops the motion of a story as effectively as a long and pointless narrative description of dog-grooming.

How you describe a field or a person's anger or a parade or a dying wish depends on your personal preferences and the story's general "feel." Sometimes dialogue is the right choice; sometimes narrative description is the right choice. Often, a combination of dialogue and narrative works best. In any case, the language should be precise, the metaphors apt, the details relevant. All good description, whether in dialogue or narrative form, should follow the rules of good writing.

TYPES OF DIALOGUE

Describing through dialogue is a challenge well worth the trouble. Different characters see things differently, and the kinds of descriptions they make tell a lot about them. Some dialogue lends itself to description better than others. *Direct dialogue*, which is the direct back-and-forth conversation between two or more characters, is not a natural vehicle for description, because many characters don't have the powers of observation necessary for conveying strong images to the readers. In the following example, Patti, an ordinary woman who works in a bakery, sounds too much like a writer to be convincing as a baker:

> "You work all night?" Gus said, surprised.
>
> "Bread doesn't bake itself," Patti said. "How do you think it gets to the shelves by six in the morning?"
>
> Gus considered this. "I'd hate working at night. It must be kind of creepy being back there all by yourself."
>
> "No, it's wonderful," Patti said. "The solitude, the pristine quiet, the aromas of yeast and flour. When I first come in I wait before turning on the lights. In that half-light I can just make out the marvelous shapes of the equipment, the subtle glint of chrome and steel, the vats of frosting arranged like sentries against the far window."

Patti sounds too self-consciously poetic here, especially after her first line of dialogue ("Bread doesn't bake itself. How do you think it gets to the shelves by six in the morning?"), which establishes her as no-nonsense and practical, not the reflective poet type who delivers the soliloquy on aromas and half-light. If you really want Patti's description of the bakery to stay in the story, consider *indirect dialogue*. Indirect dialogue paraphrases a character's words:

> "You work all night?" Gus said, surprised.
>
> "You think bread bakes itself?" Patti said. "How do you think it gets to the shelves by six in the morning?"
>
> Gus considered this. "I'd hate working at night. It must be kind of creepy being back there all by yourself."
>
> "No, it's wonderful," Patti said. She sat down and took a breath, then proceeded to describe the beauty of a bakery at night: the solitude, the pristine quiet, the aromas of yeast and flour. Even the dimness of the light seemed to charm her, for she described the shapes of the equipment, the subtle glint of chrome and steel, the vats of frosting arranged like sentries against the far window.

In this version, the poetic description is easier to swallow because Patti doesn't say the words directly. Readers won't stop to wonder whether Patti is the type who would wax poetic about "the subtle glint of chrome and steel," because the description, though attributed to Patti, belongs more to the narrative than the character. For this particular passage, indirect dialogue offers your readers the information that the bakery is, at least to Patti, a magical place. And yet you don't have to give Patti dialogue that seems too magical for her character.

Direct dialogue works best with less poetic descriptions. For example, a character named Rowe, who is describing the injuries his brother received in an accident, can do the job very well all by himself:

> "So, how's Gordon?" I asked.
>
> "Great," Rowe said, "if you don't mind sewed-shut eyes."
>
> "They sewed his eyes shut?"
>
> "It's temporary." Rowe shrugged. "Just as well, really. This way he can't see his face."
>
> I didn't want to hear it, but Rowe wasn't one to skimp on detail. "His teeth are a mess," he continued. "You ever see a whale's mouth? All the teeth look kind of chewed up and stashed back in, every which way? That's Rowe. Make you sick to look at him. The skin's all gone on the left side, nothing but raw meat."

This is a case where indirect dialogue would only dilute the impact of the raw description contained in the direct dialogue:

> I was sorry I'd asked. Rowe gave me a description of Gordon's new face—chewed-up teeth and the skin torn away, exposing raw meat. They'd sewn his eyes shut. Rowe said it was enough to make a person sick.

The indirect dialogue here robs your readers of Rowe's personality and the sense that he relishes delivering the gory details. The information seems sanitized and less immediate, because we can't hear Rowe's voice, only a third-party rendition of Rowe's voice. It's the difference between witnessing a three-alarm fire and reading about it in the paper.

Perhaps you want to tone down the gory details. You prefer a gentler rendition of the injuries. In that case, indirect dialogue is a good choice after all:

> According to Rowe, Gordon's teeth had been broken out, his eyes stitched shut, and his skin rubbed raw, as if slapped over and over by a mighty, invisible hand.

You can also combine direct and indirect dialogue as a way of enhancing certain kinds of description:

> "Look at this place," Sally said. "You're forty years old and still living in what can only be referred to as a *pad*."
> "What's wrong with it?"
> "Beaded curtains, for starters. And this album collection. Nobody collects albums. It's so retro."
> "Hey, this is a valuable collection," he said. "My Jimi Hendrix stuff alone is worth plenty." But she wouldn't quit. She recited a list of his beloved possessions as if they were character flaws: aloe plant; lava lamp; Grateful Dead poster; Indian-print slipcover; waterbed. "Are you finished?" he asked.
> She shook her head. "Honey, I'm just getting started."

In this passage, you give your readers just enough direct dialogue to show how the two characters argue. Then, in indirect dialogue (*She recited a list of his beloved possessions. . . .*) you suggest the flavor of the rest of the argument without boring everybody with a blow-by-blow. If you were to write the scene in direct dialogue from start to finish, you would dilute Sally's power, making her sound too strident or whiny:

> "Look at this place," Sally said. "You're forty years old and still living in what can only be referred to as a *pad*."
> "What's wrong with it?"
> "Beaded curtains, for starters. And this album collection. Nobody collects albums. It's so retro."
> "Hey, this is a valuable collection," he said. "My Jimi Hendrix stuff alone is worth plenty."
> "Maybe so, but look at the rest of this stuff. This lava lamp, for instance. Lava lamps went out with love beads."
> "They're back," he protested. "You see them all the time now."

"And this silly Grateful Dead poster. The Grateful Dead weren't any good twenty years ago and they're even worse now."

"Says you."

"That's right. And I say this Indian-print slipcover should take a trip to Goodwill. Maybe some needy homeless person could cut it up and use it for handkerchiefs."

"Hey, leave that alone."

"And another thing," Sally said. "This aloe plant is the stupidest thing I've ever seen. Natural medicine, my foot."

Et cetera, et cetera. Not only does Sally lose her verve, but the scene begins to bog down with too many lines of dialogue that are similar. The original passage was tighter and snappier thanks to the succinct description of the indirect dialogue.

CONVERSATIONS IN SPACE

When writing dialogue, keep in mind that readers appreciate being able to "see" where the conversation is taking place. Conversations do not occur in a vacuum; the speakers are usually doing something else—ironing clothes, starting a car, arranging flowers—while they are speaking. Also, physical surroundings can influence what characters say; a conversation held in a church might be a little more subdued than the same conversation held in a deli. To make a scene come alive, you must attend to the context of the conversation. In other words, most dialogue needs some descriptive interruption in order to make its full impact. Descriptive interruptions can take the form of a narrative break—a full-paragraph (or longer) description of a tent site in the middle of a conversation between two campers, for example—but more often these interruptions are brief and intermittent, taking the form of *dialogue tags* and *gestural pauses*.

Simple dialogue tags are the "he said/she said"'s of a dialogue sequence:

"Henry," Elizabeth said. "Tell me more."

Or:

"The car is gone!" Elmore shouted.

Or:

"Not now," I told him. "I'll explain later."

Simple dialogue tags are for identifying the speaker or implying a pause. They do not offer any description.

Dialogue tags *can* be descriptive as well as functional, however. *Descriptive dialogue tags* are tags with modifiers or modifying phrases attached:

"Those are my flowers," he said, crossly.

Or:

"Let me get it," she said, reaching for the phone.

Or:

"Just who do you think you are?" I asked, looking up.

These tags offer more than speaker identification. They describe an action or a state of mind. As a general rule, though, don't use adverbs to describe the speaker's mood. Avoid the trap of "he said, cautiously" or "she said, flirtatiously"; caution and flirtatiousness should be implied by the dialogue:

"Wait a minute," he said. "Okay, now you can light the fuse." [words imply caution]

Or:

"Why, Ricky," she said. "I do believe you're flirting with me." [words imply flirtatiousness]

The occasional, well-placed adverb is probably okay. You find them in dialogue tags written by our best writers. But you don't find them often, which makes their impact that much stronger when they do occur.

Adverbs work best in dialogue tags when the state of mind is contrary to the speaker's words:

"I got all A's," he said, glumly.

Or:

"You wrecked my car!" she said, happily.

Or:

"Why, you little creep," she said, sweetly.

Modifying phrases ("he said, reaching for the phone"; "she said, looking up") added to a tag help advance the story or provide clues about the characters' motives:

"Emily, how nice to see you again," Abner said, clenching his fists.

Or:

"Here goes nothing," Mary said, raising the sledgehammer over her head.

In the first instance, Abner's clenched fists tell us something about his feelings toward Emily. In the second instance, Mary's raising of the sledgehammer moves the story's action along.

Gestural pauses are descriptive, full-sentence interruptions that enhance or replace dialogue tags. They are similar in function to descriptive dialogue tags in that they can reveal a character's motives and move the story forward.

"Henry," Elizabeth said. She pulled her chair up close. "Tell me more."

Or:

Elmore came tearing down the street. "The car is gone!"

Or:

"Not now," I told him. I slid into the booth and ordered a beer.

How important is adding description to dialogue in the form of tags and gestural pauses? Extremely. Tags and pauses can cast a conversation in many different ways. The following conversation contains no description:

"Sally."

"I can't hear you."

"Come on, Sal, talk to me."

"I saw your mother this morning. She had some very interesting news about you."

"My mother's nuts, okay? She's off on one of her little trips to the moon. Everything that comes out of her mouth is a complete lie. It's not her fault, she can't help herself."

"Really? She seems to think she's helping you and Abby Ross plan your June wedding."

"Abby Ross? I don't even know Abby Ross. I've never even met Abby Ross. Abby Ross lives on the Foreside, for heaven's sake, what would she want with a schlup like me?"

"How long have you been seeing her?"

"Listen, I can show you the papers. I had her committed for six weeks last year. She's a pathological liar. You have to forgive them because they don't really understand all the damage they're doing."

This is direct dialogue that describes a man trying to weasel out of a tight situation. However, you can change the characters' personalities one way or another by adding description to the dialogue in the form of descriptive dialogue tags and gestural pauses:

Hank opened the screen door gingerly. "Sally."

She looked up from the flowers she was arranging. "I can't hear you," she said. She set her chin and went back to work. Dozens of roses lay in a heap at her elbow.

"Come on, Sal, talk to me."

She picked up a pair of shears and began to snip the stems. "I saw your mother this morning. She had some very interesting news about you."

"My mother's nuts, okay?" Hank said. He sidled to the far side of the kitchen, far from the sound of stems being snapped off. "She's off on one of her little trips to the moon. Everything that comes out of her mouth is a complete lie. It's not her fault, she can't help herself."

"Really?" Sally said, pointing the shears. "She seems to think she's helping you and Abby Ross plan your June wedding."

"Abby Ross? I don't even know Abby Ross. I've never even

met Abby Ross. Abby Ross lives on the Foreside, for heaven's sake, what would she want with a schlup like me?"

"How long have you been seeing her?" She held up the shears and began making little snips at the air. He moved a little farther, putting a table and a couple of chairs between them.

"Listen," he said. "I can show you the papers. I had her committed for six weeks last year. She's a pathological liar. You have to forgive them because they don't really understand all the damage they're doing."

No matter how we might have read the original dialogue, in this version we are compelled to view Sally as the one with the upper hand. She's the one with the scissors, and Hank "sidles" out of their reach. The heap of roses presents a vague impression of dead bodies, given the circumstances of her wielding the shears as a weapon. Hank shrinks from the sound of "stems being snapped off." Clearly he mistrusts his own safety in the presence of this angry woman. The dialogue becomes a cat-and-mouse game in which Hank is clearly the mouse. The description is what gives the dialogue sequence its comedic turn.

Different description choices, however, can quickly turn the mouse into a very menacing cat:

Hank burst into the kitchen and planted himself behind her. "Sally."

She looked into the sinkful of dishes. "I can't hear you."

"Come on, Sal," he said, yanking her arm. "Talk to me."

She waited a very long time, her eyes on the water, until he released her. He relaxed a little, retreated to the refrigerator to rummage for a beer. "I saw your mother this morning," she murmured. "She had some very interesting news about you."

He slammed the refrigerator door. "My mother's nuts, okay? She's off on one of her little trips to the moon. Everything that comes out of her mouth is a complete lie. It's not her fault, she can't help herself."

Sally turned, folded her arms as if steeling herself against his anger. "Really? She seems to think she's helping you and Abby Ross plan your June wedding."

Hank began to redden. "Abby Ross?" The long cords of his neck began to pulse. "I don't even know Abby Ross. I've never even met Abby Ross. Abby Ross lives on the Foreside, for heaven's sake, what would she want with a schlup like me?''

She let out a breath. "How long have you been seeing her?''

He advanced on her then, spots of sweat beginning to darken the front of his shirt. "Listen, I can show you the papers. I had her committed for six weeks last year. She's a pathological liar." She flattened herself against the sink as he lumbered over the slick linoleum. "You have to forgive them," he said, his voice dropping eerily. "They don't really understand all the damage they're doing.''

In this version, the description surrounding the dialogue gives the scene a sinister twist, *even though the dialogue is exactly the same.* Notice how the descriptions control the pace of the scene, and how that pace implies danger. If you want to slow the pace of a dialogue sequence, add descriptive interruptions. If you want to quicken the pace, use description sparingly or not at all. The first version of the preceding dialogue sequence reads at a fast, breezy clip that makes the scene feel almost lighthearted, and the last version reads slowly, with pauses implied by descriptive interruptions like "He advanced on her . . .'' or "She waited a very long time. . . .'' The result is two dramatically different scenes.

OVERDESCRIBING DIALOGUE

Be careful not to overdo it, though. Too much description in a dialogue sequence can "flood" your dialogue:

"Here's the envelope," Stanley said. He held the envelope out, his eyes fixed on the ludicrous embossed return address with the pink-tinged logo of his uncle's company.

Eleanor hesitated. She squinted up at the fluorescent lights, considering. Then she plucked the envelope from Stanley's hands, her lacquered nails gleaming. "This will be our little secret, Stanley," she said, stuffing the envelope into her purse. "I promise you, no one will ever know." She ran one deft hand across her hair.

Stanley laughed. A flat, disdainful sound. "As long as the money keeps flowing?''

Eleanor's lips parted into a thin smile. "You don't mind so much, do you?" she said soothingly. "It's Uncle's money, after all." She drew her purse closer to her coat as if daring him to take the money back.

Stanley hung his head like a bad dog. "You don't understand, Eleanor," he said, clenching his weak fists. "That's what makes it so humiliating."

She pursed her lips, inching closer to him, taking arrogant little baby steps. "Poor dear."

He shook his head, steeling himself against his own stupid tears. "I can't pay my rent," he said. He sucked in his breath and let it out slowly, his cheeks deflating. "I can't meet my child support payments. I can't even pay off a blackmailer with my own money."

Under all the hesitating and squinting and handing over and smiling and head-hanging and head-shaking and breath-taking, your dialogue is struggling to be heard. Unfortunately, the constant descriptive interruptions force your readers more than once to backtrack a line or two to figure out what question or comment the speaker is responding to. Description interruptions are most effective when inserted sparingly:

"Here's the envelope," Stanley said.

Eleanor plucked the envelope from Stanley's hands. "This will be our little secret, Stanley," she said, stuffing the envelope into her purse. "I promise you, no one will ever know."

"As long as the money keeps flowing?"

"You don't mind so much, do you?" Eleanor said. "It's Uncle's money, after all."

"You don't understand, Eleanor. That's exactly what makes it so humiliating."

She pursed her lips. "Poor dear."

"I can't pay my rent," he said. "I can't meet my child support payments. I can't even pay off a blackmailer with my own money."

See how much more dramatic this scene is without that blanket of description? In the first version you gave the readers too much guidance. Ironically, by clearing out the guideposts you made the conversation easier to follow. Your readers don't have to backtrack. And the description still delivers the crucial information—that Stanley is at Eleanor's mercy—without overwhelming the scene.

Be careful, also, about making your descriptive additions to dialogue too similar. In this first sequence, a modifying phrase follows each line of dialogue; the sequence feels rote and wooden:

> "Over here," Alan called, waving his glove.
>
> "Did I miss the game?" she asked, picking her way over the grass.
>
> "It rained. We're just now getting started," he said, giving her a kiss.
>
> "Do you expect me to stay for the whole thing?" she asked, scanning the bleachers.

In this second version, a gestural pause precedes each line of dialogue:

> Alan waved his glove. "Over here."
>
> She picked her way over the grass. "Did I miss the game?"
>
> He gave her a kiss. "It rained. We're just now getting started.
>
> She scanned the bleachers. "Do you expect me to stay for the whole thing?"

The second version is as wooden as the first, because the gestural pauses one after another seem to be following a predetermined pattern. Your best option is to combine several kinds of descriptive interruptions in the same sequence:

> "Over here."
>
> "Did I miss the game?" she asked, picking her way over the grass.
>
> "It rained," Alan said. "We're just now getting started."
>
> She scanned the bleachers. "Do you expect me to stay for the whole thing?"

In this final version, the dialogue takes center stage. The descriptive interruptions, because they are varied and therefore unobtrusive, lend shape and rhythm to the dialogue.

IMPLYING SETTING

Let's say you want to write a story in which plot and character are revealed chiefly through dialogue. Instead of explaining the setting through a descriptive interruption ("the woods were dark"), you can imply setting through dialogue:

> "These trees are beginning to suffocate me," April said. "You'd have to hold a gun to my head before I'd live here."
>
> Carrie looked around. "It's not so bad. Aunt Jean says country air's supposed to be good for you."
>
> "Air? How can air get through all these trees?" She looked up. "Your aunt must have double-sized lungs and a hell of a lot of fortitude. How can she tell day from night?"
>
> Carrie kept walking. "I think the house is at the end of this path, if I'm remembering right."
>
> "I hope she has electricity," April said. "I feel like I'm walking in the bottom of a well."

The setting implied through this dialogue is a thick woods with a house nestled somewhere therein. The beauty of implying setting through dialogue is that you allow your readers to "see" the characters—the histrionic April and tranquil Carrie—at the same time they are seeing the setting.

Make sure the characters' descriptions sound natural, and not staged for the readers' benefit. Precise description of setting shouldn't come at the expense of the characters:

> "Carrie, I'm really getting tired of walking through Ten Acre Woods looking for your Aunt Jean's house."
>
> "I think the turnoff is at the end of this path," Carrie said. "We'll just keep following it, even though it's overgrown with blackberry bushes in full bloom."
>
> April looked up. "The trees are so thick and dark. I don't like the deep Maine woods."

Both versions describe a similar circumstance: Carrie and April are walking through thick woods on a path that will eventually lead to Aunt Jean's house. The first version sounds like two people talking, and the second sounds like two people announcing. What went wrong? In the second version, the characters are describing a setting that they are too familiar with to speak of in so formal a way. So they sound like stick figures. People never make reference to what they already know. If you and a friend are walking through Ten Acre Woods, you refer to it as "here," or "this godforsaken place"—anything but Ten Acre Woods; you both already know where you are. Similarly, if you and your friend are looking for your aunt's house, you don't say, "I'm tired of looking for Aunt Jean's house," you say something like "When will we get there?" or "Do you see the house yet?" That the house in question belongs to Aunt Jean is already known to you both, so you wouldn't normally identify it any further than "the house." Similarly, the fact that the blackberry bushes are in full bloom is too obvious for Carrie to mention so precisely. She might say, "Let's get some berries" or "I just scratched my leg on that bramble," but she would not say "blackberry bushes in full bloom."

If you have to fully describe your setting early in the story, then do it through narrative:

> They were hiking through Ten Acre Woods in search of the small bungalow that belonged to Carrie's aunt Jean. It was mid-morning, but the sun was all but missing for the depth and breadth and height of the stern, ancient trees. Their path was nearly invisible, thick with blackberry bushes in full bloom, and given to false trails that forced the two women to continually double back on their tracks.
>
> "These trees are beginning to suffocate me," April said. "You'd have to hold a gun to my head before I'd live here."
>
> Carrie looked around. "It's not so bad. Aunt Jean says country air's supposed to be good for you."

The logistical details of setting are best delivered through narrative. If the interaction between characters is your main concern at the moment, you can give a general impression of the setting through dialogue and fill in the specific details a few at a time as the story progresses.

DESCRIPTION BY OMISSION

Remember the 1988 Vice-Presidential debate in which Lloyd Bentsen said to Dan Quayle, "You're no Jack Kennedy"? Everybody watching

understood that Bentsen had deeply insulted Quayle, and yet he had
not maligned his character or accused Quayle of anything untoward.
What he did was describe a man in terms of what he wasn't. This
verbal skulduggery works as well in fictional dialogue as in the real
thing.

Let's say you want a character to describe his hotel room:

> "Where did you stay?" Bernice asked.
> Izzy closed his eyes and shuddered. "You wouldn't believe
> it. The sheets were gray, the windows were gray. Even the water
> was gray. The TV didn't work and the blinds wouldn't stay down.
> I stayed awake all night squashing cockroaches."

In this description, you give your readers a vivid picture of the hotel
poor Izzy stayed in. You can conjure an equally memorable picture
by describing the place in terms of what it wasn't:

> "Where did you stay?" Bernice asked.
> Izzy closed his eyes and shuddered. "Let's just say it wasn't
> the Hilton."
> Bernice waved him away. "The Hilton's overrated, in my
> opinion."
> "At least they fumigate once in a while," Izzy said. "And
> you don't get rashes from the shower, last time I checked."

In the revision, you invite your readers to imagine much more than
the specific details of the first version. The fact that Izzy's hotel "isn't
the Hilton" evokes opposite images: rude personnel instead of polite,
wrinkled sheets instead of ironed, and so on. Also, Izzy's contention
that at the Hilton "they fumigate once in a while" and "you don't
get rashes from the shower" creates images at least as horrible as the
ones in the first version. We can picture armies of bugs marching
over a soggy, balding carpet, and a shower with inches of mildew and
who-knows-what-else clinging to the walls. All this, and Izzy hasn't
actually said one word about the place; he's talking about the Hilton.

This technique works well when a character is describing people, too:

> Mac watched my daughter make her way from one end of
> the pool to the other. "Not exactly Esther Williams," he said,

"but then again she's only nine."

Or:

> "Who's our new boss?" I asked.
> "Remember Arthur?"
> "Yeah," I said. "The man was an angel."
> "Let me make this clear," Alice said, leaning close to my face. "Our new boss is not Arthur. Not even close."

The unsaid is a powerful tool. It can be used in narrative description as well ("Linden Island was not the tropical paradise the group had been led to expect from the travel guide . . ."), but direct dialogue is its most natural venue. After all, people are prone to use description by omission, whether they are sipping tea in a restaurant or participating in a nationally televised debate.

WRAP-UP

Description and dialogue often overlap. Your characters can describe in four lines of dialogue something that might take you two paragraphs of narrative to convey. Neither dialogue nor narrative description is an inherently better technique; which choice you make depends on the individual scene. If you want a breezy, fast-paced scene, then use a lot of dialogue and a little description. If you want to slow the pace of a scene, then add descriptive interruptions to your dialogue. Descriptive interruptions can add comedy or suspense or poignancy to a scene, because they guide the readers' perceptions in a way straight dialogue—which can be interpreted in many ways—cannot.

Dialogue can be direct—

> "I'm pregnant, everybody!" Kristen announced

—or indirect:

> Kristen announced that she was pregnant.

Direct dialogue generally delivers a better sense of a character's personality, but indirect dialogue can give you more room to use your own language for description:

> Holding on to her blossoming belly, Kristen announced her pregnancy in a voice loud enough to fell a moose.

A combination of direct and indirect dialogue usually makes for a natural-sounding exchange between two characters, especially if the scene is long and filled with details that don't warrant their own lines of dialogue:

> "I hate your mother," he said, "because she's Polish."
> Then he went on to malign my Italian grandfather, my Jewish brother-in-law, and my English aunts.

Descriptive interruptions almost always enhance a dialogue sequence, because conversations do not take place in a vacuum. People talk while shaving, moving furniture, scaling mountains, and mailing letters. These descriptive interruptions sometimes come as full narrative breaks, but more often take the briefer form of *dialogue tags* and *gestural pauses.*

Simple dialogue tags ("he said/she said") identify speakers and imply pauses. *Descriptive dialogue tags* describe a character's actions and/or state of mind:

> "Not in this lifetime," he said, heaving the body overboard.

Descriptive tags like this keep the action going while the characters are conversing. Avoid adding single adverbs to dialogue tags ("he said, angrily"; "she said, sadly"); the state of mind should be implied in the dialogue itself or in the ensuing action. You shouldn't have to explain the meaning of a line by adding crossly/avidly/sadly/happily.

Gestural pauses are full-sentence interruptions in dialogue that enhance or replace dialogue tags:

> "I heard you, Ivan," Millicent said. She waved him away. "But you'll have to wait."

These pauses usually describe a gesture that delivers information about a character's mood or motives.

Dialogue tags and gestural pauses can control the pace and even the meaning of a dialogue sequence, but they can also smother the dialogue if used too frequently. Also, be sure not to use the same kind of tag or pause with each line of dialogue—the conversation will appear wooden. Look up an author whose use of dialogue you admire. Chances are you'll find some lines tagged, some modified with a phrase or full-sentence pause, and many others left to stand alone.

You can use dialogue to imply setting without having to make a full-scale description of a place or event. A line like

"My God, this place looks like the dark side of the moon," Henrietta said,

can replace a whole paragraph of narrative description. You can also imply setting by what a character doesn't say about it. A line like

"It's not exactly Sesame Street," Brenda murmured,

can describe the mean streets of a large city without mention of broken windows and bloodstained concrete. Be careful not to "stage" dialogue only for the readers' benefit, though. "Let's climb the glass-strewn stairs of my three-story apartment building" sounds more like an announcement to the readers than part of a conversation. People never make mention of what they already know; if the broken glass and three stories are important, you'll have to find another way to reveal them.

Think of dialogue as a description technique. Good dialogue, like all good description, should help you move your story forward, illuminate your characters, and enrich your readers' perceptions of the story.

CHAPTER 5

DESCRIPTION AND POINT OF VIEW

POINT OF VIEW IS THE PERSPECTIVE from which a story is told. It is the single most important choice you make for your story. More than any other technique, point of view influences how readers perceive the story you are trying to tell.

Which character is my main character? Which character do I want readers to empathize with and understand? How do I want readers to view the setting? All these questions can be answered by your choice of point of view.

When point of view is well chosen and firmly in place, the story hums along, seemingly all by itself. When point of view falters, the story loses its focus, its momentum, its reason for being. Point of view is the glue that holds a story together; it also dictates what kind of description you may use and which characters get to do the describing.

Imagine the story of Cinderella in the wicked stepmother's point of view, or Dickens's *A Christmas Carol* narrated by one of the ghosts. The wicked stepmother wouldn't be able to see her own wickedness or Cinderella's smudged beauty, and the Ghost of Christmas Yet to Come wouldn't give a hoot about the parlor games in the home of Scrooge's nephew. Point of view heavily influences description; different perspectives bring out vastly different aspects of a story.

For beginning writers especially, point of view can be difficult to grasp; it requires constant attention. Point of view becomes less intimidating with experience, but its problems haunt every writer at one time or another, no matter how accomplished or experienced he or she may be.

Point of view comes in three forms: first person, second person, and third person. You have a few other choices within these three categories.

FIRST-PERSON POINT OF VIEW

Beginning story writers love to employ the first-person narrator, a common and useful technique for creating immediate, seductive, captivating fiction. The trouble comes when the story's narrator is too closely based on the author. A reader pauses: Is this fiction, or an essay, or what? It's true that most of us began writing by writing about ourselves, and that an author's life often yields engaging and even powerful writing. But fiction is its own discipline; you might even say it's more challenging than non-fiction, because you have to invent a life before you can begin to interpret it.

The Narrator Is Not You

To make the first person work effectively, keep one thought in mind: *The narrator is not you.* An essay is not a short story. A memoir is not a novel. In fiction, the first-person narrator is a *character you create.* Since you have created him and decided to let him tell the story, it is your duty to remember that he is no one but himself. Allow him his own voice, his own beliefs, his own eccentricities, however distant they may be from your own. Think of the first-person narrator as your chance to be somebody else for a while, like an actor playing a role.

The problem of author-as-narrator is only compounded when the events being described in the story "actually happened." Real-life events rendered as fiction almost always fail, because our editing radar doesn't work very well with stories too close to our own experience. We end up putting everything in, because everything that happened to us in this particular scenario is remembered as important. The softies among us may also take out key scenes so as not to hurt Mom's or Uncle Bill's feelings. If you must fictionalize an actual event, then take the point of view of someone else involved in the event and use him or her as your narrator. Take a key item and change it dramatically—a lost love becomes a lost job, a plane crash becomes a fender-bender, a pet dog becomes a herd of sheep. You can mine the emotional territory that interests you while inventing fiction that is fresh and new.

The worst defense for a failed story is "It really happened."

You may not like your first-person narrator, and that's fine. Let her talk. She has a story to tell in her own way; the worst thing you can do to her story is impose yourself on it. Don't be afraid your son will think you had a short career as a loan shark. Or, worse, that your readers will think you're a bigot, with a mouth like the one on the narrator you've created. This is one of a writer's occupational hazards. Don't censor your narrators! (Mom will understand.) If a reader insists that your narrator is you, then score one for your descriptive powers.

Once you've established a proper distance between the first-person narrator and yourself, and between yourself and the events being narrated, your challenge isn't over. In fact, it's just beginning. First-person narration comes with problems—some enjoyable, some aggravating, all of them approachable. Let's begin with the problem of observation.

The First-Person Narrator As Observer

The first-person narrator is, above all else, an observer. A first-person narrative has a distinctive "voice"; voice becomes character, character becomes story. But what makes that voice worth listening to? Sometimes it is the grammatical miscues and syntactical detours that define a voice—regional idioms, occupational buzz words, grammatical pyrotechnics—but even a narrator with a quirky voice is not interesting unless he or she has a good story to tell. Celie, the narrator (by way of letters to God and her sister) of Alice Walker's *The Color Purple,* has a distinctive grammar, but what makes her so compelling is the way she observes her world:

> Us dress Squeak like she a white woman, only her clothes patch. She got on a starch and iron dress, high heel shoes with scuffs, and a old hat somebody give Shug. Us give her a old pocketbook look like a quilt and a little black bible. Us wash her hair and git all the grease out, then I put it up in two plaits

that cross over her head. Us bathe her so clean she smell like a good clean floor.

This passage is breathtaking not simply because of the "accent" of the speaker, but because of her acute and telling observations. What she chooses to observe tells us a lot about her world. Her similes make use of the homely objects within her own grasp. The pocket-book looks like a quilt; the clean smells like a floor.

Holden Caulfield, narrator of J.D. Salinger's *The Catcher in the Rye*, reveals himself similarly:

> This family that you could tell just came out of some church were walking right in front of me—a father, a mother, and a little kid about six years old. They looked sort of poor. The father had on one of those pearl-gray hats that poor guys wear a lot when they want to look sharp. He and his wife were just walking along, talking, not paying any attention to their kid. The kid was swell. He was walking in the street, instead of on the sidewalk, but right next to the curb. He was making out like he was walking a very straight line, the way kids do, and the whole time he kept singing and humming.

Holden's slang, which is a delight to listen to, pins him to a certain age and era, but what makes him real is his series of heartbreaking observations. He finds sorrow and poignancy and pathos everywhere, especially in children. "Kids' notebooks kill me," he tells us after reading his little sister's. Describing a boy who fell out a window, he says,

> Finally, what he did, instead of taking back what he said, he jumped out the window. I was in the *shower* and all, and even *I* could hear him land outside. But I just thought something fell out the window, a radio or a desk or something, not a *boy* or anything.

Through his distinctive observations, Holden reveals his own alienation and despair.

The trick of making a first-person narrator's observations authentic is to make sure that the narrator speaks from his own experience. Holden's use of the phrase "poor guys" clues us to the fact that he is one of the "rich guys." Celie's "clean floor" shows us something about her unadorned world. A different kind of narrator might compare that clean smell to newly printed money. A narrator other than Holden might not have noticed the child's walking in a straight line, but rather the cut of the child's coat. Consider the differences in the following line delivered by different narrators:

> Sandra's son reminded me of a prince, only more imperious.

Or:

> Sandra's kid looked kind of like my cousin Gino, only loads cuter.

Or:

> Sandra's little boy reminded me of that boy in the shelter, only fatter, and a cleaner face.

Or:

> Sandra's boy reminded me of a hush puppy, only stupider and higher strung.

All of these narrators have a set of experiences and prejudices and obsessions that is unique to them. As their author you must allow them their own visions.

Lest you become too discouraged, remember that the "right" observations don't come in the first and second drafts. It takes almost as long to get to know a fictional person as it does a real person. For example, you may not know how your narrator would observe a flooded basement until you have seen her in other situations. In the first draft, she would probably see the flooded basement in more or less the way you would see it:

> I stuttered down the steps, groping for the light. I grabbed the pull-chain and cursed out loud at what the light revealed. Two feet of water, enough to unloose my books from their shelves. They drifted languidly on the water's surface, darkening horribly as the grainy water crept up their innocent spines.

This is the observation of a narrator who loves books. Clearly, she is pained to see the books in such a state. The word "spines," though it obviously refers to book spines, feels strangely human, as if the narrator were imagining herself in the creeping water. The books seem to have a life of their own, drifting "languidly." Through this keenly observed moment, you show your readers something about the narrator. But this is only a first draft; you have no idea who this person really is. What if it turns out, by the end of the story, that the floating books is the only suggestion that this woman has an intellectual life? Perhaps the story is all about her compulsion to keep this flooded house in the best possible condition so that she can sell it out from under her two-timing husband. Three or four drafts later, this woman has become much more solid in your mind. Her single-minded vindictiveness fascinates you. You go back through the scenes, scouring the piece for false notes, and the flooded basement is the first alarm. Books? This woman, you suddenly realize, hasn't read a book since she was sixteen. Even if there were books floating around down there, she wouldn't see them in this panicky way. She would have a completely different view from yours:

> I stuttered down the stairs, groping for the light. I grabbed the pull-chain and nearly laughed out loud at what the light revealed. Books. A little marina of books floating on at least two feet of grimy water, some of them sinking already, some of them light enough to float forever. There must have been a hundred of them, all Barry's silly books he'd kept from college, bobbing like mini ice floes in the basement of the house I resolved right then and there would be sold before summer. I kicked one with my foot. Getting to the sump pump was going to be a problem.

In this revision, the narrator doesn't have any feeling for the books except as a hindrance to her action. In the first draft you had no way of knowing this, so you "filled in" with observations of your own. Now you have no choice but to muster the fortitude to *go back and erase yourself from the first-person narrator's experience*, to allow the story to be hers and hers alone.

Good first-person observation rests on imagination—your ability to envision how one particular character might perceive the world around him. To observe through another's eyes takes practice, and this is one area in which writing exercises actually help. Try describing a car wreck from the perspective of five different passers-by: one might notice the blood, another the dented hood ornament, another the stunned face of the driver. Imagine how each of them might be standing, or breathing; what inaudible words might be escaping their lips? Imagine where they might just have come from, or where they are on their way to. A funeral? A playground? Put on their clothes, take up their space on the sidewalk, and then, looking through their eyes, write what you see.

First Person and the Child Narrator

Creating a first-person narrator is a special joy as long as you remember that every sprig of description, every observation, belongs to that narrator alone. This "ownership" becomes a particular challenge when your narrator is a child. Sometimes it seems as if your only choice is between some Dickensian orphan and the precocious little brother on a television sitcom. Don't despair; your choices are actually endless, as varied as the number of children in the world. The challenge is to find one child's unique voice, a voice readers are willing to believe.

If you are in the habit of listening to real-life children, however, you see your problem. Who, really, wants to listen to a 10-year-old (unless he's yours) tell a story of any considerable length, with his pauses and detours, faulty logic, limited insight and vocabulary, and self-absorbed world view? The trick is to make the child seem ten (good luck working with a first-person narrator any younger than that) while giving him the gifts a good storyteller needs. Remember the fundamentals—the telling detail, simile and metaphor, use of the senses—and keep the language simple:

> For a second I wasn't sure it was really Grandma in that bed. At first I thought maybe she was a ghost, but the hissing turned out to be her trying to breathe. There was something wrong with her skin, little cracks all over, like somebody dipped a spider's feet in red paint and let him walk on her. Her mouth left a wrinkled little hole where her teeth were supposed to be. "Hey, Grandma," I said. "It's me, Freddy!" She looked right at me with grandma eyes and that's when I knew it was her.

The passage is descriptive in several ways. You convey a physical picture of the dying woman; you suggest the child's fear (the hissing) that eventually gives way to his natural enthusiasm (the sudden dialogue); and you add a poignant little punch when he recognizes "grandma eyes." This is a sophisticated picture rendered in language that befits a ten-year-old.

You want to avoid fancy vocabulary, of course, but don't underestimate your narrator, either. Some child narrators end up sounding like this:

> I looked in the bed but I wasn't sure it was Grandma. She sounded just like a big, scary ghost 'cause it was hard to breathe. Boy was I scared. Her face was marked all over with little red lines that looked just like spider legs. And she didn't have her teeth in, so her mouth was real tiny and wrinkly. "Hey, Grandma," I said. "It's me, Freddy!" She looked at me real slow. Her eyes were just like Grandma's, so I knew it was her.

This second example probably sounds more like a "real life" 10-year-old, but "real life" dialogue rarely translates well. You have to manipulate it to make it sound real on the page. Don't shortchange your child narrator. He can manage complex sentences and good rhythms as well as any adult. Keep the vocabulary simple, don't skimp on metaphor (he can handle that, too), and let him talk.

First Person and the Reminiscent Narrator

The reminiscent narrator is an adult looking back on a turning-point experience, usually one from childhood or early adulthood. Your challenge and responsibility as the writer is to make sure the description doesn't get too mushy. Reminiscence is dangerous stuff; the reminiscent narrator treads the fine line between sentiment and sentimentality. In the following example the adult narrator tells the story of his father's dying, back when the narrator was ten years old:

> I was sadder than I had ever been before, looking out the window of the room where my father lay dying. He was trying to sing my song, but he was so sick by then he couldn't bring it off. My heart sank and I fought back tears as I listened. Finally I ran to him and threw myself on the bed and hugged him as hard as I could, fighting back a river of tears.

This narrative manipulates readers into feeling sad, because it takes a pretty hard heart not to be moved by these circumstances. But the passage is nothing more than cheap melodrama, with the clichés of sinking hearts and rivers of tears. And notice that the passage contains not one concrete image: it is simply an explanation of how the narrator felt, in abstractions. Compare this to the following passage, which is from the end of "Leo," a short story by Sharon Sheehe Stark:

> From behind me came a thin strand of sound, low and broken. I thought he was moaning and, frozen, I could not turn to him at first. Minutes passed, the rain drummed down, and in the same instant I recognized the tune, it came to me, like shocking news, that on this day of measured time I, Jeremiah, was still a child. I left the window and went to him, driving myself tight against the bony harp that was my father's body. He went on humming my song, stopping often for breath, until we both went to sleep.

In this profoundly moving passage, specific detail summons our deepest emotions. The "thin strand of sound," the "bony harp," the "stopping often for breath" are things we see and hear and feel. This narrator never tells us that he still faces a well of grief over a long-ago death; rather, he leads us through his experience as if it were our own, and this is what makes the story so unforgettable. When treading deeply emotional material, your reminiscent narrator must rely not on easy abstractions ("I was sadder than I had ever been") but on fresh, specific, and relevant details. By embracing the specific you can usually keep yourself clear of melodrama. Tears and heartaches are a dime a dozen and touch us only briefly; the image of a "bony harp" is unique and touches us forever. Don't aim to make your readers cry. Aim to make them remember.

First Person and Physical Description

How the first-person narrator observes the world is one matter; how he observes himself is another, much thornier matter that has flummoxed inexperienced writers since forever. How does a first-person narrator describe herself? Let's say a character named Julia is a physically beautiful woman, for reasons that are important to your story.

In the third person, you can describe Julia as thoroughly as you wish without sounding self-conscious:

> Julia fidgeted at the study carrel on the third floor of the library, winding a strand of auburn hair around her finger. She had the look of a Botticelli maiden, her wide, flat face composed and pale, delicate blue veins pulsing under the translucent skin of her brow.

Try converting the above passage to first person and see what happens. What you get is a cloying, self-indulgent passage that begins, "I fidgeted at the study carrel" and goes on to say, "I had the look of a Botticelli maiden," ending with, ". . . the translucent skin of my brow." What a drastically different character from the ingenuous young woman reading in the library!

The physical description of a first-person narrator presents a perplexing problem that has more than one solution. Try some of the following solutions to see which techniques best fit the purposes of your story.

Let the narrator describe herself outright. A first-person narrator can sometimes describe herself without resorting to the self-indulgence of the preceding example. It's up to you to find a descriptive tone that fits the narrator's personality. How direct you allow the narrator to be depends on what kind of character you wish to create.

A wry, self-confident Julia might describe herself this way:

> Because I'm red-haired and grey-eyed and fond of tight clothes, men keep mistaking me for their old girlfriends. "Wanda!" they'll holler, charging across the street, against the light. "Marlene? Is that you?" they'll ask, scanning my chest as if looking for a name tag.

A narrator like this one reveals not only her appearance, but her personality. We expect an unsentimental story from a self-confident woman. Although she hasn't come right out and said it, she obviously appreciates her own good looks. She doesn't tell us that "some men" or "most men" look at her. "Men" look at her; in fact, they risk life and limb to get to her side of the street! A narrator like this is a true challenge—she demands a linguistic flair that you must sustain over the dozen or so pages of a short story. You have to give this version of Julia a rollicking syntax and quick wit in order to do justice to her *joie de vivre*. She's got pizazz, so the writing's got to have a little extra fizz, too.

A less confident Julia might sound more like this:

> At the finishing school I attended in my nineteenth year, Jessica Lange was the rage. Meryl Streep, Kathleen Turner. Blonde was in. My hair was a blemish they were too polite to mention, like a scar or leg brace. I was the only girl in my dorm who didn't have call-waiting. "Redhead," my roommate would whisper mournfully when describing me to a potential blind date.

Here we have the beginnings of a physical description from a different kind of storyteller. In this version of Julia, her wryness is tempered by a certain restraint. She sounds reserved (". . . in my nineteenth year . . ."); indeed, she sounds like the product of a finishing school. We may expect a bit of self-deprecating humor (the last line could be tongue-in-cheek, we don't quite know yet), but that humor will exist only in the context of longing or reflection.

Self-description does not have to contain wryness or irony to sound natural. As long as there is a logical reason for self-description, even the most self-effacing character can get away with it. Let's reinvent Julia yet again. This time she is just beginning to emerge from a shut-away life:

> After my father died I lost one hundred and twenty pounds—a whole person—and my true face began to appear: the high cheekbones I remembered from my youth, the grey eyes larger somehow in so much less flesh. Even my hair seemed more prominent—red and curly—now that my extra face was gone.

Here Julia is solemn and reflective; we don't expect pizazz. We expect a more thoughtful, even meandering story, something that matches Julia's reflective tone. Her self-description, though direct, has a chilling subtext, because Julia is really talking about an emotional metamorphosis, not a physical one.

Use description by association. If your first-person narrator is not the type to describe herself at all, then you've got to get sneaky. How about letting her compare herself to someone else? In the following example, Julia is shy and confiding; you can let her speak of her beauty this way:

> I have my mother's hair, thick and red. She used to braid it for me, her trembly fingers sifting the strands as I stood before her, paying attention. I have her eyes, too, grey and wide set, and her pinked lips. I inherited her face when what I wanted was her spirit.

In this version, we infer Julia's beauty from the unusual coloring and the fact that she's comparing herself with her mother, who has "spirit," which is a form of beauty all by itself. Because she is speaking of her appearance in terms of inherited traits, the self-description seems neither too self-conscious nor too self-congratulatory. After all, she has nothing to do with her looks, she got them from her mother. Do you see how you have slipped Julia's appearance into her own narrative while offering your readers some clues to her personality? She remembers her mother lovingly, and looks back on her childhood with benevolence.

Notice also how you've woven in the phrase "paying attention"; it's an evocative phrasing that probably has something to do with the emotional content of the story. Maybe Julia missed something after all: she didn't pay *enough* attention. Or, maybe something she did pay attention to at her mother's knee is now coming back to help or hinder her. Remember, always: *Description is rarely used for its own sake, but to present a story in a certain way.* If Julia had been "wriggling and writhing" instead of "paying attention," then you would have yet another version of Julia on your hands.

You needn't stick with family members to make associative descriptions. Consider this example:

> Bobby was Irish, I was Italian. Though our appearance was a study in contrasts (his hair was flame orange, mine so black it looked blue), we were both poor and in need of longer pants, so our teachers often took us for brothers.

Notice that the narrator's description draws on ethnic proclivities that paint a vivid picture. Because their hair color is described in such extremes, we know that Bobby looks not just Irish, but very Irish, and that the narrator looks not just Italian, but very Italian. Doesn't it go without saying that Bobby's eyes are blue, his skin pale? That the narrator's skin is dark, his eyes brown, maybe even black?

Besides giving your readers a physical description of the narrator, you give your story a powerful context. Ethnic differences contrasted with economic similarities is evocative and intriguing, hinting at a rich and complex story.

Use your plot. If a certain physical feature—a scar, a limp, baldness, obesity—is important to the plot, then your best bet is to introduce it in context:

> Because I had always been the biggest kid in the class, I was accustomed to being last in line.

Or:

> I boarded the bus (jammed as usual) and scanned the faces. Usually there was at least one—a wizened grandmother or a good-natured child—who didn't mind sharing space with a white man.

Or:

> "One life jacket," Jamie murmured. "Only one of us can jump."
>
> Frank's eyes flew open. "But we'll die on board. The boat is sinking!"
>
> "We have ten minutes, tops," Jamie said evenly. "Who's it going to be?"
>
> Each of them slid a resentful little glance my way, and I leaned on my crutches with a thrill of defiance.

In the first example, the narrator is a loser who attributes his bad luck to his large size. In the second, the narrator is a stranger in a strange land, whose color is the heart of the story. In the third example, the narrator's handicap will become his triumph as he uses it to manipulate his comrades into saving his life. In each example, the physical characteristic contributes to the story: *because* he's big, he's always last; *because* he's white, he encounters hostility; *because* he's on crutches, he is resented but saved. The physical description feels natural because it is essential to the plot.

The observant second party. Let another character do the narrator's work for her. Observant second parties can point out a bad dye job or a club foot more naturally than the narrator can—they are on the outside looking in. The observer can describe directly, or the narrator can report what the observer says. Careful here. A report like "He told me I was the most exotic, breathtaking beauty he had ever seen" makes the narrator look bad, unless she is being ironic or naive. Consider the following examples, which use second parties who are in a position to observe Julia:

> My mother was always telling me how pretty I was, how grey my eyes, how red my hair, the color of rusted fall leaves, she said. I carried myself like a queen, she said, over and over, like a preemptive strike against the neighborhood boys who might not share her enthusiasm. To my sister, whose beauty went without saying, she offered nothing at all.

Or:

> "Where did you get those pretty grey eyes?" Mrs. Lawson cooed, her plump and dimpled self bent over to look me in the face. Her own eyes loomed large, blue and full of questions. I backed up, not knowing what to say. Where did eyes come from? I retreated to my playhouse, away from Mrs. Lawson and all the other adults who pelted me daily with questions to which I didn't know the answers.

Or:

> "I wish I had your hair," my sister sighed. "Red is all the rage right now." She laughed. "You're finally in style, Julia."
> "Imagine that," I said dully. I knew what she was up to.
> "Of course we'll have to cut it. It's too long the way it is now. Too heavy." She lifted the front of my hair as if parting a curtain.

In each of these examples the physical description is parceled out only as it belongs to and illuminates the story. The first example reveals a daughter's remembrance of her own appearance, but more important, her mother's indulgence; the second example reveals a child's appearance, but more important, that child's terror of the ordinary adult world; the third example reveals a woman's appearance, but more important, her combative relationship with her sister.

You may have your own solutions for describing a first-person narrator, or you may use a combination of the above solutions, which overlap anyway. Be careful, however, of solutions that seem too easy. In the rush to get a story down, you might be tempted to resort to hackneyed devices, which do nothing for your story except mark it as a beginner's. The following suggestions should keep you out of trouble.

Avoid the mirror. In the mirror technique, the narrator is passing by a hall mirror, or shaving in front of the bathroom mirror, or catching a glimpse of himself in a storefront just about the time a physical description is in order. "A haunted face stared back at me." "I saw a woman with grey eyes and red hair." "I realized I still had blood on my face." This device isn't always bad—sometimes a character can be effectively startled by his own appearance—but often it feels too obvious, and besides, it's been done to death. Unless the mirror is an integral part of the story, such as a magic mirror, a vain narrator, avoid using it.

Avoid the overly observant second party. This solution is what you get when you try too hard. "But you're so beautiful!" the *overly* observant second party might say. "Those lovely grey eyes, and that thick, auburn hair you inherited from your mother. Your slim waist and delicate hands. How can you think you're plain?" Unless the observant friend has an urgent reason to be going on like this, the description looks staged, calls attention to itself, turns the observer into a nitwit, and robs the narrator of her own voice. You must constantly remind yourself how people really speak. "You're so beautiful!" a second party might reasonably say, but would she include the color, texture, and origin of the hair, the color of the eyes, the look of the hands and waist? Not likely. Let the observant second party gush over Julia's beauty if she must, but slip in the specific details with a subtler stroke, using the aforementioned solutions.

Avoid staged details. We've discussed this already, but it bears repeating: Don't stage details for the readers. Details of physical appearance should appear *naturally* in the story, not like this:

> Joe drew his gun. I backed up, clutching at the loose strands of my ash-blond hair.

Goodness, your readers ask, this woman's about to die and she's telling us what her hair looks like? First-person narrators almost never "just happen" to think of their hair or eye color, or their height or girth or anything else. Usually they are fixed *outward*, on what they themselves are seeing, not what others are seeing in them. If you find yourself placing physical details at illogical spots in your story, go back to the above "good" solutions for physical description.

FIRST-PERSON POINT OF VIEW

- An "I" narrator tells the story himself or herself.
- The "I" narrator is not the author; you must erase yourself from your narrator's experience!
- Allow the "I" narrator his own quirks, prejudices, and vocabulary.
- Make sure the "I" narrator's observations fit with her world. A professional skater might call the night sky "black as ice"; a printer might call the same sky "black as ink."
- When the narrator is a child, simplify the vocabulary but don't necessarily drop all imagery from the prose. A child sees in simile, too: "The dog was big as a bear."
- When the narrator is an adult looking back (a reminiscent narrator), watch for sentimentality. Avoid cliché. Use the specific in place of the abstract. Replace indistinct feelings ("I felt nervous") with something the reader can see or feel or hear: "Every tick of the clock sounded like a gunshot."
- If you want the reader to get a physical picture of the narrator, be careful about letting the narrator describe himself. Don't use mirrors, ponds, or storefronts to let the narrator see himself and relay what he sees to the reader.
- The "I" narrator should describe himself only if the descrip-

tion also reveals his personality: "I admit I was a handsome devil." Otherwise, try the following techniques:

1. Describe by association: "I'm husky like my sister."
2. Use the plot: "Because I was tall she put me last in line."
3. Use an observant second party: "I thought you'd look much older," he said.

SECOND-PERSON POINT OF VIEW

The second-person point of view isn't used much, probably because it's a bit strange—not the way readers are used to having stories presented to them. Also, second person can begin to feel cloying or gimmicky over the space of a long story or a novel. Not that it can't be done: Jay McInerney uncovered the full potential of second-person point of view in his novel *Bright Lights, Big City*. Lorrie Moore used second person to great advantage in her story collection *Self-Help*.

Second person is often used as a glorified first person, as if the first-person narrator were talking to herself:

> Because you're red-haired and grey-eyed and fond of tight clothes, men keep mistaking you for their old girlfriends. "Wanda!" they'll holler, charging across the street, against the light. "Marlene? Is that you?" they'll ask, scanning your chest as if looking for a name tag.

Notice that the descriptive style is exactly the same as in the first-person point of view. You can't inject your own comments or observations; the story belongs entirely to the second-person narrator.

The second-person narrator has a bit more leeway than the first-person narrator when it comes to physical description. For one thing, the confident second-person tone implies a certain degree of chutzpa: the narrator is almost always infused with self-confidence:

> You sidle up to the teller's window and run a hand through your thick black curls. She's yours already. She likes the dimple

in your chin, even the creases that have lately turned up near your eyes when you smile.

If you transpose the above passage to first person, the character sounds unacceptably obnoxious. Second person gives the readers just enough distance to accept this kind of self-description from a character.

The second-person point of view is usually rendered in present tense, perhaps because present tense reinforces that second-person sense of urgency. Ordinary observations seem weightier somehow when transposed from first to second person. The smallest details take on extra gravity, and you can add tiny descriptive touches that you can't get away with in first person:

> **First person:** I peer into my husband's musty study. The clock I stole from Mr. Bloom is still ticking, its square and gloomy face revealing nothing.
>
> **Second person:** You peer into your dead husband's study. The clock you stole from Mr. Bloom is still ticking, its square and gloomy face revealing nothing.

In second person the description of the clock takes on more ominousness, and you are also free to add the adjective "dead." The word "dead" in the first-person version of this passage would have seemed too staged, as if you had planted it there only for the readers' information. In the second-person version, it fits right in with the weighty feel of that point of view.

SECOND-PERSON POINT OF VIEW

- "You" is the stand-in for the "I" narrator: "You walked into your cozy little house and some blond had eaten all your porridge."
- The story belongs to the "you" character just as if he were a first-person narrator. Keep the details true to the "you" character's experience.
- Careful not to let the "you" character sound like an outtake from a Humphrey Bogart movie. The second-person tone can

easily slip into hard-boiled-detective mode: "You approach the door. You knock. You turn the knob. You hold your breath." Vary your sentence constructions to avoid this pitfall. Don't start every sentence with "you," any more than you'd start every sentence with "I" in a first-person story.

- Physical description is easy to bring off with a "you" character, because second person strikes a confident tone: "You decide to wear the red raincoat because it makes you look like Liza Minelli on a good day."

THIRD PERSON OMNISCIENT POINT OF VIEW

Third-person narration can take various forms, depending on how close you want your readers to get to your characters. Third-person narrative is traditionally divided into two broad categories: *omniscient* point of view and *third-person-limited* point of view. In *omniscient narrative*, a (usually) disembodied, all-knowing "voice" tells the story. Some omniscient voices have so much personality that they seem to be characters themselves:

> Our darling heroine's words, spoken in a frail tremor that could turn the blackest heart inside out, resonated through the choir loft like the final notes of a hymn.

The momentary dip into first person ("our darling heroine") is a nineteenth-century convention that is little used today. Nevertheless, omniscient narrators can be fully present even when they do not announce themselves so overtly:

> Angel Callahan, a plump, silly woman with a thicket of graying hair, lumbered across the lane like one of the sloe-eyed sheep she was so fond of herding.

Other omniscient narrators are nearly invisible; the story seems to have appeared fully formed on the page, unaided by hand or voice:

> Randall pressed the envelope closed, the tips of his fingers

whitening as he mashed them against the gluey flap. His siblings watched, their eyes glittering darkly.

The omniscient narrator may enter the mind of all the characters, in a "God's eye view":

> The contents of Randall's envelope scared Jill, intrigued Marty, and disgusted Joan.

Or, the narrator may remain objective—a mere "camera eye view" that reports events without entering the characters' heads:

> Randall sealed the envelope as his siblings watched. All the faces in the room reflected varying degrees of anger.

Or, the narrator may confine omniscience to one character, in a "focused omniscience":

> Randall Gardner was a shrewd, unfeeling man with a flair for the dramatic. The morning shadows slatted across his back as he bent languorously over the writing table. He sealed the envelope with a theatrical flick of the fingers, aware of the dark glow of his siblings' glittering eyes. That he had no idea what they were thinking was his first failure of the day.

As you can see from these examples, the omniscient narrator has great latitude. The omniscient "eye" may roam all over a story, from character to character, place to place, past to present to future. The omniscient "voice" may interpret events or merely record them. And, unlike the first-person narrator or third-person-limited narrator, the omniscient narrator has the entire English language at his disposal. (I use "he" for simplicity's sake, though the narrator is more of an "it" that a "he" or "she.") The omniscient narrator can use language as formal or casual as he wishes, regardless of the characters whose story he is telling.

These point-of-view choices affect the readers' mental image in different ways. The omniscient narrator may give us a perception of the events and also a feeling or attitude about those events. Or, the omniscient narrator may be so invisible as to grant us only the barest information that we must then make our own judgments about. What we perceive depends on the nature of the omniscient narrator.

Omniscience is tricky business; the trick is finding the narrative style and tone that fit the story and then keeping that style and tone consistent. As the preceding examples show, omniscient narrators don't all sound the same. It is up to you to find the omniscient voice that fits the story's purpose. Consider the following first lines:

> **Example One:** Once upon a time . . .
> **Example Two:** Upstate New York.
> August 1906.
> Half-moon and a wrack of gray clouds.
> Church windows and thirty nuns singing the Night Office in Gregorian chant. Matins. Lauds. And then silence.
> **Example Three:** Who that cares much to know the history of man, and how the mysterious mixture behaves under the varying experiments of Time, has not dwelt, at least briefly, on the life of Saint Theresa, has not smiled with some gentleness at the thought of the little girl walking forth one morning hand-in-hand with her still smaller brother, to go and seek martyrdom in the country of the Moors?

The first example is the opening line of countless fairy tales; the second is the opening of Ron Hansen's short novel *Mariette in Ecstasy*; the third is the first line of George Eliot's great novel *Middlemarch*. From these first lines, we understand something about the type of story we are about to hear. The omniscient narrator makes a pact with readers from the outset: Settle in; listen; I know everything and will relate it in a certain way and in due course. The omniscient voice—that is, the descriptive style—is established immediately and profoundly affects the way we perceive the story.

The omniscient narrator often has a perspective—sometimes subtle, sometimes overt—on the story being related. He may even insert opinions from time to time. In *The Portrait of a Lady*, Henry James describes his main character this way:

> Isabel Archer was a young person of many theories; her imagination was remarkably active. It had been her fortune to possess a finer mind than most of the persons among whom her lot was cast; to have a larger perception of surrounding facts, and to care for knowledge that was tinged with the unfamiliar.

It is clear that this omniscient narrator (who in the opening of the novel even refers to himself as "I" and then disappears gradually as the story unfolds and Isabel becomes the primary focus) has opinions about all kinds of things, including Isabel's qualities and those of her contemporaries. The omniscient narrator must, above all, carry an air of authority. This is true whether you choose a fully present omniscient narrator or an invisible one. Readers must feel they are in the hands of the expert, the one who knows everything there is to know about the story in question, and who plans to relate the story in exactly the order, style, and method it was intended to be told.

The Omniscient Tone

Assuming this authority is a great challenge to the writer. Because the omniscient narrator has access to every character's background, disposition, and inner thoughts, and may choose to reveal any or all of these things at any given time, a writer can become overwhelmed with too much choice. Keep reminding yourself that what unifies the omniscient narrative (or any narrative, for that matter) is consistency of descriptive style. Beginning writers often believe they are writing in the omniscient point of view, but a lack of consistency mars the overall tone so vital to a convincing omniscient narrative. For example, if you present the daughter in your story as "juked on quaaludes, tippy-tappin' her painted toes, and singin' man-oh-man like a cat in heat" and two pages later describe the father as "a midwestern gentleman of portly stature and possessed of a heart burdened by melancholy," the unlucky readers are left to puzzle over a host of characters in search of a narrator.

The following examples illustrate how the right descriptive style can unify tone. This is the opening of a story about Anna Tremblay, a spoiled debutante who has just returned from a charity mission in Central America.

> Anna's welcome-back party was just getting started. Her mouth dried when she saw Ralph walk in. She slunk behind one of the beaded curtains to look him over. His puppylike features were crossed with misgiving. He was worried about seeming too eager or too casual—he still couldn't believe that Anna had spent six weeks helping to build a health clinic in God-Knows-Where. Evelyn had filled him in on the tantalizing details, though he made a point of believing only a quarter of anything

Evelyn had to say. Marcus, standing by the punch bowl and clutching his wife's silk purse, squinted at the party-goers with disdain. "These people don't give a hoot about Anna," he told his wife. "They're just hoping for some virtue by association." His wife nodded; she agreed with everything her husband said not because she loved him but because she was afraid of him.

Whoa! Whose party is this, anyway? Beginning writers, thinking they are telling a story with an "objective" (i.e., omniscient) narrator, make the mistake of jumping from character to character because an omniscient narrator is allowed to. (A little like climbing a mountain because it is there.) The problem is, the above passage *has* no omniscient narrator. In fact, there is no narrator at all, just a bunch of characters clamoring for center stage. There isn't much description, either, you'll notice. A narrator doesn't simply *relate* a story, he or she *describes* a story. The omniscient narrator should assume a certain perspective and stay with it—think of omniscience as the same music playing in the background from beginning to end. Let's try this party again, this time with an omniscient narrator who, while not a character himself, lends a definite perspective to the story.

Because they liked to be seen every four or five weeks, everyone on Park Place Drive turned out for Anna Tremblay's welcome-home party. Anna, determined to appear a free spirit, had her father's drawing room cleared of furniture and decorated with eight hundred tiny straw dolls strung on wire so thin they appeared to be dancing on air. The effect was frivolous and frightening all at the same time, much like the pastel facades of the Park Place houses.

At eight-thirty Ralph Plunkett arrived, the imperious rustle of his trenchcoat vibrating strangely in the cavernous, empty room. Anna offered her hand—ringless, sunburned, slivered from six selfless weeks of hammer-and-nails in Guatemala—like some exotic hors d'oeuvre; Ralph hesitated only a moment before he impulsively kissed it. "Welcome back," he said, then looked up as a flurry of other guests appeared at the door. The Stillwaters, the Coopers, the Smythes, the Jernigans, coiffed and bejewelled, their tinkling laughter swirling around a subtle core of malice. Anna greeted them all, extending that same unpolished hand, that naked, exotic thing, her prize.

In this second version of the party, the prose is unified by a central voice, an omniscient presence that sees the entire neighborhood and describes the events with a pointedly arched eyebrow. Although we don't yet know who the central character is going to be (by the third or fourth paragraph, we *should* know, however), what *is* clear is that the story contains themes of class, pretension, deception, and that the storyteller has an opinion about them. The details are more specific and meaningful than those in the first version, and every word seems to flow from the same consciousness. The piece is so convincingly unified by perspective and tone that the word "selfless" has to be taken as condescension and nothing else.

An omniscient narrator may love or hate his characters, but he is rarely neutral. The pathos or ridicule or humor in a story lies in the way the omniscient narrator chooses to describe events. The tone may be casual or formal, humorous or grave, admiring or condescending. These perspectives are revealed through such innocent devices as adjectives, verbs, adverbs, syntax, even punctuation.

The omniscient narrator above describes Anna as "*determined to appear* a free spirit," which alerts the readers to Anna's smugness and self-delusion. How differently would we perceive Anna had the narrator observed, "Anna *was* a free spirit"? Why, we might actually believe that her Guatemalan trip was selfless. To strengthen the notion of Anna's self-delusion, the narrator describes the party decor not as "lots of South American decorations" but, rather, as the specific "eight hundred tiny straw dolls strung on wire. . . ." This accuracy of detail not only gives us a better sense of the absurd decor (and the personality of Anna and the whole neighborhood), but also gives Anna away by revealing the number of dolls as if she had counted them herself. Some free spirit! It is clear that Anna has thrown much time and thought into this party, that she wants to be perceived in a certain way. The narrator tells us that her efforts are "frivolous and frightening all at the same time, much like the pastel facades of the Park Place houses." We understand immediately that the story will be about more than a neighborhood party, because a certain tone has been set. The final line, which refers to Anna's scarred hand as her "prize," gives away the narrator's perspective: Anna is a rich girl who thinks six weeks of work is a badge of courage, and she's going to milk it for all it's worth.

Notice, too, the imagery that the omniscient narrator uses; it is loaded with meaning. The room is "cavernous, empty," much like the characters' lives. Ralph's coat makes an "imperious rustle," which calls to mind the very rich and the presumption of power. The image of the straw dolls seeming to dance on air is powerful in the context of Anna's artifice—is she any more substantial than one of those dolls? The description here is careful, relevant, accurate, and consistent in tone—this is how omniscient narrators are created. This narrator doesn't miss a thing, and the story he is handing to the readers is deftly layered with his interpretation of events.

Omniscience and Physical Description

In the omniscient narrative, physical description of characters is not very restrictive. Knock yourself out. Compare the main character to Jack Ruby or a burrowing mole or Princess Grace. It's your show. The omniscient narrator sees everything however he wishes to see it. You needn't worry about violating a character's point of view, because the point of view does not belong to the character in an omniscient narrative; it belongs to the voice or presence that is telling the tale. What you do need to watch for, however, is the omniscient narrative's consistency with itself. The above story would strike a false note if Anna Tremblay were compared to a "beauty-parlor groupie, all hair goop and Mary Kay." The references to "goop" and "Mary Kay" would be out of step with this omniscient narrator's arch, sophisticated vocabulary. You could use the same comparison with slightly different wording:

> Her excellent address notwithstanding, Anna always looked as if she'd just stepped out of a beauty parlor down on Third Avenue, in full violation of the unspoken rule that a sophisticated woman's hair should not be as wide as it is high.

Obviously Anna herself would never offer such a description; nor would Ralph or the other guests at the party. The omniscient narrator has a wonderful freedom with physical description that can be a lot of fun for the writer. This freedom of description is an omniscient narrative's best virtue, making its other challenges well worth the trouble.

Omniscience and Child Characters

Child narrators can be effective storytellers (see the section on first-person point of view), but what if you don't want your child character to tell her own story? She might not have the language to express her complicated situation; perhaps something takes place in the story (a secret adoption, or a plot to kidnap her) that the child can't know about; or maybe the story must be told in an arch tone that is contrary to the child's nature. A switch to omniscience will instantly solve all problems of child voice and child tone and child perception; what you sacrifice, however, is proximity to the child.

When you convert a first-person narrative to an omniscient narrative, you begin to write a different story altogether, whether you want to or not. You sacrifice the child's wide-eyed descriptions for a more sophisticated (but often more lyrical, more satisfying) description from an omniscient narrator. Look at the following examples:

> **First person:** Momma's going away today. I know because Auntie Rita told me. I was sitting on Momma's big trunk and Auntie Rita scooched down to look at me. I smelled lipstick on her mouth, and little sparkles of powder showed on her face when she smiled. . . .
>
> **Omniscient:** It was Rita who had to tell the child that her mother was going away. The child sat on the lip of the great packing trunk, her spindly legs hanging over the edge, the heels of her Mary Janes tick-ticking against the lock. Rita squatted awkwardly on the balding carpet and looked into the child's light-filled eyes. Rita smiled. "Honey . . ." she began. But that was all. Aunt and niece remained still in the buttery light, their mouths locked against questions they dared not ask or answer.

If you are willing to forego the first-person immediacy of the child's experience, you often end up with a richer story with more shades of meaning in the descriptions. In the second version the child's perspective is gone, and yet the heartbreak of the scene remains, aided by buttery light and locked mouths and ticking shoes. The "tick-ticking" shoes suggest not only a child's fidgety demeanor but the excruciating passage of time: the child has only a few more moments before her mother leaves. Similarly, their "locked" mouths suggest not only an inability to speak at the present moment, but a sense that this moment itself will be "locked"—locked into the child's memory, locked out of future conversations. A child narrator cannot convincingly deliver this kind of description herself.

Sometimes a story demands an intimacy with the character that omniscience cannot provide. Without resorting to first-person narration, you want to draw your readers deep into the character's experience. This is where third-person-limited point of view comes in.

THIRD-PERSON-LIMITED POINT OF VIEW

The other type of third-person narrative is the *third-person-limited consciousness* (some call it *third-person central intelligence*, or *third-person central consciousness*). This point of view, which we'll call *third-person-limited*, has a somewhat omniscient feel, but breaks from omniscience in that it works from *inside* the character. The story must follow the point-of-view character's version of events.

Omniscience works from the outside in; even if the omniscient narrator concerns himself with only one character, he is still free to rove around and observe things that the character can't see. In third-person-limited, however, *the readers are not allowed to perceive or observe anything that the main character cannot perceive or observe*, which somewhat limits the kinds of description you may use.

Look again at this example from the section on omniscient point of view:

> Randall Gardner was a shrewd, unfeeling man with a flair for the dramatic. The morning shadows slatted across his back as he bent languorously over the writing table. He sealed the envelope with a theatrical flick of the fingers, aware of the dark glow of his siblings' glittering eyes. That he had no idea what they were thinking was his first failure of the day.

In order to convert this passage from omniscient to third-person-limited point of view, we must alter it considerably:

> Randall liked to use his flair for the dramatic. He bent languorously over the writing table and sealed the envelope with a theatrical flick of the fingers, aware of the dark glow of his

siblings' glittering eyes. That he had no idea what they were thinking was his first failure of the day.

The third-person-limited narrator *inhabits the character's body.* Randall has no way of seeing slats of light on his own back, so we cannot put those slats of light into the description. Ralph does not think of himself as shrewd and unfeeling, so we must find other ways to suggest these character flaws. These limitations can be pesky, but they're well worth the trouble if your goal is to give readers an intimate bond with the character.

Because the third-person-limited narrative confines itself to the consciousness of only one character, its style has certain limits. The description—the similes and adjectives and metaphors—must contain imagery that exists in the realm of the character whose story is being told. Remember, in omniscience you're working from the outside in—"Emily's rain-soaked hair stuck to her bare back in gummy, webbed tendrils"—and in third-person-limited you're working from the inside out—"Emily's rain-soaked hair felt like cold snakes on her back."

In third-person-limited point of view, the readers are not *looking* at a character, they are *inhabiting* a character. For this reason, it's a good choice for short fiction, bringing the readers immediately into a character's world and holding them there until the last word. Take a look at a recent issue of fiction magazines like *Story* or *Glimmer Train*; chances are you'll find a preponderance of third-person-limited point of view.

Degree of Intimacy in Third-Person-Limited

The omniscient point of view comes with choices: God's eye view, camera eye view, and focused omniscience. Third-person-limited also contains choices, though fewer of them. There is only one category of choice, really: degree of intimacy (John Gardner called it "psychic distance"). For example, you may choose a very intimate third-person-limited point of view, in which the descriptions match the character's vocabulary, ethnicity, socio-economic status, prejudices, and world view. The third-person-limited narrative voice sounds almost as confiding as a first-person narrator, as if you were merely repeating

what the point-of-view character would have said herself. The degree
of intimacy with the character, in this case, is great. In a less intimate
third-person-limited point of view, you still remain inside that character's experience, taking care that the readers see or hear nothing
that the character can't see or hear, but the language you use to
convey that experience is more sophisticated or lyrical. In this case,
the degree of intimacy is distant.

Let's experiment with varying degrees of intimacy in the following passage about an undereducated Oklahoma teenager who is witness to her father's arrest for car theft:

> **First person:** I couldn't believe they was coming for Daddy.
> I set to hollering my head off and banging my feet so hard on
> the porch you could see sparks flying off the heels of my shoes.
> I thought maybe I could scare them police away, but it didn't
> work, they come for him anyway; when Daddy held out those
> poor bony wrists I had to shut my eyes against the sunlight
> screeching off those big steel cuffs.

> **Third-person-limited (intimate):** Emmy couldn't believe
> they were coming for Daddy. She set to hollering her head off
> and banging her feet so hard on the porch you could see sparks
> flying off the heels of her shoes. She thought maybe she could
> scare the police away, but it didn't work, they came for him
> anyway; when Daddy held out those poor bony wrists she had
> to shut her eyes against the sunlight screeching off those big
> steel cuffs.

> [*Notice that the grammar is corrected, but the description is exactly
> the same and her father is still referred to as "Daddy."*]

> **Third-person-limited (less intimate):** Emmy couldn't be-
> lieve they were coming for her father. She began hollering her
> head off and banging her feet so hard on the porch you could
> see sparks flying off the heels of her shoes. She thought maybe
> she could scare the police away, but it didn't work, they came
> for him anyway; when her father held out those poor bony wrists
> she had to shut her eyes against the sunlight screeching off those
> big steel cuffs.

> [*Notice that the father is now "her father" instead of "Daddy,"
> and "set to" is changed to "began." The character's actual voice is
> beginning to disappear, though the readers are still experiencing the story
> from inside the character.*]

Third-person-limited (distanced): Emmy couldn't believe they were coming for her father. She began to shout and holler, stamping her feet so hard that sparks appeared between her shoes and the floorboards. She was hoping she could scare the police away, but they came for him anyway; when her father held out his poor bony wrists she had to shut her eyes against the sunlight glancing off the officer's cruel-looking handcuffs.

[*Notice how the language has gone more formal, though we are still inside Emmy's experience. One more step away and we'd be looking at her from the outside, that is, with an omniscient narrator.*]

The above examples show you the restrictions of language in third-person-limited. You can work close in or far away, but the perspective must be the character's and not the narrator's. If you wanted to make the above passage a little more descriptive by adding a simile, be careful how you choose. You might end up making a mistake like this:

. . . the light glanced off the steel cuffs with the unbearable brightness of an African desert.

Oh, really? And where might Emmy, a farm kid from Oklahoma, have seen this African desert? Okay, on TV maybe, but your readers might stop to wonder. What you have done here is announce your presence as the author by violating the readers' intimate connection to Emmy's mind and heart. An image so foreign to Emmy's experience forces us to suddenly look at Emmy from the outside in. Emmy might compare the glare of the handcuffs to sunlight on waves of grain, or a shimmer of heat lightning, or the morning sun glancing off the silo. But African deserts are too far out of her realm to be plausible; it violates our belief that we are moving through Emmy's world.

Each character, no matter what her circumstances, has a store of imagery at her disposal. It's up to you to root it out. The third-person-limited narrator must remain invisible; the character is the only presence. You may take liberties with grammar and style, but the way the character sees the world is the way you must see the world, for now. (Save your own visions for an omniscient narrator.) Far from enriching the story, description that is foreign to the character's life merely calls attention to itself.

Physical Description in Third-Person-Limited

The problems of physical description in third-person-limited are almost identical to those in first person. Remember, in third-person-limited you must keep the readers inside the body of the character; therefore, you cannot allow a description like this:

> Patty watched the elevator doors groan open. Alan was standing inside, smirking, the manuscript he'd stolen from her tucked into a leather binder. She watched with disbelief as he lifted one manicured finger to beckon her inside. She felt her breath escape in small stutters through her closing throat. "You," she said, but the word dried on her tongue. Blood swirled in her head and her pulse banged against her temples. "Going up?" he asked. Her brown eyes blackened with rage.

Up until the last line, "Her brown eyes blackened with rage," you have your readers firmly planted inside Patty's consciousness. Then, suddenly, you ask them to jump outside Patty's perspective for just long enough to look at her brown eyes. The readers may not be able to identify just why, but they will feel momentarily distanced from the story. Do you see how the description falters with that one line? You've moved us from the inside to the outside. If you *must* provide a physical description of Patty, then go back to the beginning of this chapter and try some of the physical-description techniques for first-person narrators. Some of those techniques work beautifully in third-person-limited. For instance, in this scene you have access to an *observant second party*:

> The elevator doors opened. "Hello, Brown Eyes," Alan
> said.

Or, you could use *description by association*:

> She studied him carefully., His hair was a vague no-color, his skin dull and cold. Prison pallor, they'd laughingly called it when she worked here. Too many fluorescent lights. She liked to think she no longer looked like that. She liked to think her skin had recovered its Italian glow, that the blue highlights had returned to the dark of her hair.

Or, you could *use your plot*:

> They got off at the fifteenth floor, where a platoon of blonde secretaries marched in and out of glass-fronted offices. Patty sighed. How had she ever fit into this place, where being a brunette was considered a handicap?

When writing in third-person-limited point of view, remember, always, to *work from the inside out, not the outside in.*

Third-Person-Limited and Child Characters

The old theater maxim "Never work with children or animals" could also be applied to writing fiction. Children and animals register on the melodrama meter almost before you've written a word. They turn out too cute or too smart or too forlorn or too mischievous or too something. In the section on first-person point of view, we explored ways to allow child narrators to tell their own stories convincingly. In the section on omniscient point of view, we saw that omniscient narrators can more fully tell a child's story, but the downside is the readers' loss of intimacy with the child. Third-person-limited gives you the best of both: you allow your readers to experience the child's world without having to shackle yourself to the child's language.

Let's look again at Freddy, the first-person narrator we heard from in the section on first-person point of view. Freddy is ten years old, looking in on his dying grandmother:

> For a second I wasn't sure it was really Grandma in that bed. At first I thought maybe she was a ghost, but the hissing turned out to be her trying to breathe. There was something wrong with her skin, little cracks all over, like somebody dipped a spider's feet in red paint and let him walk on her. . . .

First-person narration works quite well for this character, but a third-person-limited narration would grant you more leeway with language:

> Freddy stole up the steps, his heart thump-thumping against his ears. The door before him seemed achingly large, thick with paint. Grandma's sick, they had told him, but what did they mean? He held out one palm—the fingers still stained

with blueberry juice—and pushed. The door groaned open and there she was, white and weightless as a feather. The skin over her temple was webbed and pulsing, nearly translucent. "Hey, Grandma," he whispered. "It's me, Freddy." She turned to look at him. Freddy nearly cried out with relief to see those familiar Grandma eyes, blue as ice. She moved her lips but he couldn't hear her over the sound of his hammering heart.

In the above passage the language is sophisticated and lyrical, not language Freddy himself would use, and yet the description is true to Freddy's experience and vision. The similes—using feathers and ice—are taken from objects in Freddy's world. The readers see nothing that Freddy does not see, hear nothing that Freddy does not hear; the passage is filtered through Freddy's consciousness and his alone. And yet the storyteller is someone other than Freddy, a nearly invisible vehicle that presents Freddy's story to the readers. You as the author have preserved Freddy's child-ness without sacrificing your natural descriptive style. This freedom of language is what makes the third-person-limited point of view so satisfying.

Of course, you may decide to limit your description to a more intimate third-person-limited view, and come up with something like this:

Freddy looked into the bed but he wasn't sure it was Grandma. She sounded just like a big, scary ghost because it was hard for her to breathe. He was so scared! Grandma's face was marked all over with little red lines that looked just like spider legs. . . .

However, why use Freddy's language when you don't have to? If you're going to restrict the language of the story to a ten-year-old's abilities, then you might as well leave the story in the first person.

THIRD-PERSON POINT OF VIEW

Third-person point of view takes two forms: *omniscient point of view* and *third-person-limited point of view.*

Omniscient point of view comes in three styles:

- GOD'S EYE VIEW
    1. The storyteller sees all the action—even action that the characters can't see—and sometimes expresses opinions about it.
    2. The storyteller knows all the characters' thoughts and feelings, and can move from one character's "head" to another's.
    3. The omniscient narration is always in third person, unless the narrator is God, or a magic dog, or a ghost, all of which are problematic, to say the least.
    4. The narrative contains a tone of authority that unifies the story. ("Once upon a time there were three bears. . . .") Readers feel they are in the hands of a reliable storyteller who will deliver all the relevant aspects of the story in the proper order.

- CAMERA EYE VIEW
    1. The storyteller sees all the action, but does not know the characters' thoughts and feelings.
    2. The storyteller has no opinions about characters or events. The story is reported but not interpreted.
    3. The camera-eye view makes for a distanced narrative, and can become frustrating to the reader if the story is a long one.

- FOCUSED OMNISCIENCE
    1. The omniscient storyteller sees all the action, but enters only one character's thoughts and feelings.

Third-person-limited is the other kind of third-person point of view.

- The story is told in third person, but through only ONE character's point of view.
- The reader is not privy to anything that is outside this one character's sight or hearing. The reader knows only what this character knows.
- In third-person-limited, the reader experiences the character from the inside out: "The rain made Emily's hair feel like cold snakes on her back." The reader is made to feel he or she is inhabiting the point-of-view character's body.

WRAP-UP

Good description flows from point of view, and vice versa. When determining point of view for your next story, remember your choices: first person, second person, and third person. The first-person point of view requires an engaging and convincing narrator. The second-person narrative has a distinctive tone and offers you slightly more descriptive latitude than first person. The third-person point of view offers you the most descriptive freedom. You may use an omniscient narrator who has access to any and all characters, who may or may not express opinions, and who may reveal as much or as little of a character, or characters, as he likes. The third-person-limited narrator, on the other hand, has access to only one character, and may not venture outside that character's perspective or reveal anything that the point-of-view character does not see, feel, or know.

Once you have a good grasp of the limits and freedoms of the various points of view, be sure to match the descriptive style to the point of view you have chosen. Children see the world differently from adults; old people have a different vocabulary than young people. An invisible omniscient narrator adopts a more formal tone than a fully present omniscient narrator. An educated first-person narrator has a different speaking style than an uneducated one. A third-person-limited narrative can be so distant as to feel nearly omniscient, or so intimate as to feel a half-step removed from first person.

Physical descriptions of your characters should not violate point of view. These details must emerge as a natural part of the story and not simply as information for the readers' benefit. Be careful also to separate yourself from your narrators, whether or not they are in first person. The "I" or "Eye" telling the story is not really you, it is a character you create.

Don't be discouraged if you have to refer back to this chapter many times before point of view becomes second nature. It is a problem of craft that even the most experienced writers grapple with again and again.

CHAPTER 6

DESCRIPTION AND STYLE

A WRITER'S STYLE IS COMPOSED of hundreds of choices big and small, from point of view to sentence length to word choice. As you work through the first drafts of a story, you should be struggling with certain questions: Is the main character the right one? Am I using the best point of view? Does the structure enhance or hinder the story's progress? Do I need more scenes and less narrative? Should I change tense? Are the paragraphs too long or too short or too similar? Am I using too many modifiers or too few? These questions help you form your descriptive style.

If you have already "found your style," however, and always write in a certain way, these questions become moot. If you always write in present tense with nineteen-year-old narrators who favor compound sentences, your stories may eventually run out of energy and start sounding alike. Examine any writer's body of work and you will find stylistic changes (some of them dramatic) between the early work and the later. Try to stay open to changes in your own style, to keep yourself interested in and challenged by your own writing.

Many inexperienced writers overlook the fact that style evolves as much from the characters as from their creator. A style that suits the first novel may wreck the second, because the characters in the second novel see the world differently from the characters in the first novel. Wedding yourself too soon to a writing style can squelch your natural instincts for adventure and experimentation. Think of the hundreds of characters you might never meet!

CHOOSING DESCRIPTIVE STYLE

In a first draft we don't yet know our characters or fully understand the situation we have placed them in. The first draft of a story usually has a vague shape, an approximation of a beginning, middle, and end, and a theme that is barely discernible. The only thing we can literally "see" in a first draft is the writing style. Florid or bare-bones, it is there on the page. Perhaps because we are so grateful at this stage to have *something* we can see, we are reluctant to alter the style that brought us the gift of a first draft. In subsequent drafts we may change the main character, manipulate the plot, alter the sequence of events, add scenes and jettison others—but the original style we leave alone. Why? Doesn't it stand to reason that changes in plot or character should affect style? Writers often forget to go back and check for stylistic harmony, and yet that harmony is the very thing that gives a story its final polish.

Let's analyze descriptive style through some examples. A first-draft passage set in a rural backwater might sound like this:

> **Version One:** Franny sat on the porch, cracking one knuckle after another, squinting out at the ragged, dusty stretch of asphalt that passed for a road. Tuckered and heat-weary, she hissed a ribbon of air through her lips. Her brother Emmett was on his way, so they told her, but she'd believe it when she saw his mud-ugly face and not one minute before.

This descriptive style is peppered with imagery in keeping with a rural setting. But what if you decided, midway through the fifth draft, that your story about this estranged brother and sister would be better served in a more suburban setting? Fine, you say, let's move the story from Rural Route 1 to a Cape Cod-style house on Maple Street:

> **Version Two:** Franny sat in the breezeway of her mother's neat white Cape, cracking one knuckle after another, squinting out at the sedate blacktop of Maple Street. Tuckered and heat-weary, she hissed a ribbon of air through her lips. Her brother Emmett was on his way, so they told her, but she'd believe it when she saw his mud-ugly face and not one minute before.

Something is suddenly wrong with this picture. The stylistic flourishes don't work in a non-rural setting. Phrases like "tuckered and heat-weary" and "mud-ugly" clang against the ears. Down-home phraseology doesn't sound right unless the setting is down-home.

It is nearly impossible to change a story without altering style at least a little; even if the characters are essentially the same, they have a different address now. The story requires a different descriptive tack:

> **Version Three:** Franny sat in the breezeway of her mother's neat white Cape, cracking one knuckle after another, squinting out at the sedate blacktop of Maple Street. The trees, fully leafed, seemed vaguely military, lined up and staring. She cast her eyes down, letting a noisy ribbon of air escape her lips. Her brother Emmett was on his way, so they told her, but she'd believe it when she saw his unwelcome face and not one minute before.

Can you see the style evolving into something else as the story changes? The first version, with its dust and heat, conjures expectations of ancient family feuds set amidst the unforgiving southern landscape. The second version, with its suburban setting and down-home phrasings, conjures a variety of expectations that don't go together very well. The third version suggests a subtler, more tightly controlled family conflict, with its military imagery and sophisticated language.

By the fifteenth draft you may decide that the rural setting is more in keeping with the story's intentions after all. By this time, however, you've developed a style that feels comfortable to you: a present-tense omniscient narrator with a "writerly" vocabulary. The lyricism feels true to the story's lofty theme of betrayal and forgiveness. Do you have to alter the style again in order to go back to the original setting? Probably not, if this is indeed your fifteenth draft. The style is solid enough by now that it can withstand a change in setting:

> **Final Version:** Franny sits on the splintered porch rail, draping her bare legs over the edge. They dangle like ropes: long, delicately knotted, burnished by the sun. Her fingers, too, are long, and she works one hand over the other, her knuckles making chips of sound in the hot, empty day . . .

This passage seems more whole, more finished, than any of the other examples. The down-home phraseology is gone, but the poetic language that replaces it evokes a hot country day just as effectively. The prose is delicate and strong at the same time, like the character you are describing. The individual images are gentle—"draping her legs," "delicately knotted," "chips of sound." And yet the resulting picture—the actual thing being described by these images—is a strong, knuckle-cracking, sunburned young woman. Here is a person of limited prospects who has the potential to do something extraordinary when faced with a family conflict. Style and content harmonize, and the story feels finished.

As you can see by the number of examples here, stylistic harmony rarely happens by accident. You have to play with different kinds of description, over a great number of drafts, before you discover the right notes. This is not a matter of "hitting" the right style, like turning a roulette wheel and hoping for a black seven. Style develops, little by little, as you work a story through its paces. So, don't be in too much of a hurry. Your goal, after all, is not to make the writing effortless, but to make it seem effortless. That marvelous fraud is achieved only one way—through relentless hard work.

WHEN CONTENT AND STYLE CONTRAST

Style does not always have to match a story's content. You can describe ragged people in tidy prose. You can describe a corporate takeover in the comfortable slang of a night watchman. Sometimes, a contrast between style and content works to a story's advantage. The opening of *A Wrestling Season*, a novel by Sharon Sheehe Stark, presents a simple situation. Trover, a middle-aged lawyer, does not want to go to his father's funeral. His wife makes him go anyway:

> In the end, of course, they all went, as Trover knew they would from the start. He knew as much even as he addled and deviled and danced his dances. . . . What was he if not a hostage, as always, in the heart of his own family? As they peeled out between the two large fields, he noted dimly the plucked and stubbled landscape and that their man Sprecher was out in the cold, mowing yellow grass. Wasn't this November? Wasn't it

going to snow? And how suddenly open the land was, haze in the distance, the horizon revoked and nothing, *nothing*, mediating between him and the unopposable outwardness of things. He closed his eyes.

The surface of this situation is ordinary enough, but the author's lyrical style infuses this ordinary character with an almost mystical quality. We understand that Trover is a man capable of depth and feeling no matter what his outward appearance may show.

Marlene Buono, in her short story "Offerings," does something similar, only in reverse. The situation in the story is mystical, but prose is simple. The two-page story gives us a woman who collects apologies, placing them in her pockets, sewing them into her hems, fashioning them into paper birds. The story ends with a visit to her husband's grave:

> She opened the hatbox she had brought along and lifted out an apology that she had meant to give her husband before he died. It was an awkward shape and she rarely looked at it because it filled her with shame. She deftly folded the edges until the perimeter of the regret was smooth. Emily studied the apology before each fold, carefully coaxing it to forget its graceless form and accept her design.
>
> She took an hour to give it the wingspan it needed. When she placed the finished apology on the tombstone she watched it unfold its wings and fly.

In the first example, an ordinary situation is made magical with lyrical description. Here, a surreal situation is made accessible by direct, unadorned description. We understand that Emily has an ordinary person's regrets and sorrows, no matter how extraordinary her actions seem on the surface. In each case, the story's heart is revealed through contrast.

Whether to contrast content and style depends on your intention for the story. Suppose you are writing about a vivacious, successful actress who will discover, over the course of the story, that she has lived life only through her stage roles and that her real life is little more than empty gesture. A bubbling, florid style would match her outward appearance, but a pared-down style would honor the subtext, which is the emptiness of her soul. Let's try the pared-down style first:

Version One: Esmerelda stood outside the theater, studying her own image. The poster was finely printed and resembled the old-fashioned movie posters her friends were fond of framing for their living rooms. Her hair in the poster was blonder than in real life. Her smile was broader. Her fingers were longer. The poster was no mirror. She could not see herself there.

This style creates an intriguing narrative tension. Something is just slightly askew here; the character does not quite fit the spare prose that describes her. You're implying a seriousness, even a foreboding—a hint that the journey of this story will turn inward, perhaps in ways that Esmerelda is not ready for. Even her extravagant name is made more ordinary in the context of these simple sentences and everyday words. This descriptive contrast invites the readers to peer behind Esmerelda's glitzy facade.

A more flamboyant description, one that is more in keeping with Esmerelda's outward exuberance, delivers a somewhat different expectation:

Version Two: Esmerelda skittered over the dirty Forty-fourth Street sidewalk in shapely black stiletto heels, listening to the sparks of sound that followed her like an echo. She stopped just below the lighted marquee, the sequins on her dress making shimmering tracks along her body as she moved under the light. She gazed at the poster that bore her own image. Blonder, longer-limbed, infinitely happier, her poster self smiled into the night with the arrogance of a Park Avenue pigeon. *Go around me,* her poster self seemed to say, glinting strands of hair flying away from her head like molting feathers. *Just try to make me move.* The other Esmerelda, the flesh-and-blood Esmerelda, the Esmerelda who had spent four tumultuous hours deciding on a dress, lifted her face to the marquee and fixed her eyes straight into the icy light of a hundred tiny moons.

In this version, which features long, looping sentences and lots of imagery, there is not much contrast between who Esmerelda is and how you present her. This already flamboyant character becomes larger than life, promising a big, bright story. Careful, though: an oversized character combined with oversized prose might be too much for the readers to swallow. Esmerelda might end up looking like a character in a soap opera.

Let's make another try at contrasting style and content in this story about an ordinary supermarket clerk:

> **Version One:** Abigail dragged a box of cornflakes across the scanner and let it float down the stainless-steel chute. Spreading her fingers, she palmed a dappled cantaloupe and swept it twice over the tiny window until she heard the beep. She watched the cantaloupe roll down behind the box, squat and graceless and yet possessed of a liquid slow motion. Next, she hefted a can of peas, its multicolored label pulsing with images of nature's bounty. Everything today was color and shape: the dangerous red of the Cortlands, the tidy domes of the egg cartons.

Here, a lyrical style contrasts with a mundane setting. Readers get a sense that something extraordinary might happen to a girl who sees beauty in a can of peas. Notice how much movement you've built into the description: the box "floats"; the label "pulses"; the cantaloupe is "possessed of a liquid motion." Notice also the colors and shapes: "squat and graceless"; "dappled cantaloupe"; "dangerous red"; "tidy domes." What a feast for the senses! The readers prepare for a story in which something interesting is going to happen, no matter how little potential the character, an ordinary check-out clerk, seems to have.

What happens if you match style and content here?

> **Version Two:** Abigail scanned several items: a box of cornflakes, a can of peas, two cartons of eggs. Then she scanned a pound of fish, a bottle of bleach, and a bag of apples. She watched the scanner light up with each pass of her hand.

This pared-down style dulls an already dull situation. What happened to Abigail, who had so much promise just a moment ago? She disappeared along with the descriptive flourishes. This passage contains no adjectives, no adverbs, no color, no sound. Content and style match too well: the result is a monochromatic description, the literary equivalent of a one-color painting.

A CASE FOR MINIMALISM

Never has a descriptive style been revered and maligned as much as minimalism. Minimalism, which is currently out of fashion due to overexposure, has never been satisfactorily defined. To most writers, minimalism means short and spare. The story is barely told; the readers are supposed to read between the lines. A minimalist story requires strong details and a compelling main character. The characters are usually ordinary working stiffs dealing with life's ordinary slings and arrows. Some critics dubbed these stories "Kmart fiction" because of some minimalists' tendency to use brand names of places and products as a shorthand for characterization. (A character's use of Aqua Velva is supposed to suggest his age, income, and value system, for example.) The best of these writers, however—Raymond Carver, Ann Beattie, Mary Robison, Amy Hempill—do indeed paint complex pictures with only a few strokes. They dig in and find exactly the right details to reveal character without resorting to brand-name characterizations.

Minimalism suits many beginning writers because it fares well with simple, one- or two-character stories. This is not to say that writing minimally is easy. It only *looks* easy. In fact, minimalist stories are hard to write and easy to parody. The second version of our story about Abigail the grocery clerk, for instance, is a parody of minimalism. The readers are supposed to "read between the lines" to find meaning in a list of grocery items. Many short-story writers of the seventies and eighties adopted this no-frills descriptive style in an attempt to imitate the great minimalist writers, most notably Raymond Carver. (I wrote some imitations myself, I'm sorry to say.) What we forgot—in our rush to flatter our elders in the sincerest form possible—is that for a story to hold up under this style it must be *inherently interesting*. When prose is this minimal, you have no place to hide.

If your natural writing style tends toward minimalism, do not despair. Attention to descriptive style can turn a monochromatic story into minimalism at its best. The smallest adjustments in the grocery-item passage, for example, can infuse even a spare story with a sense of expectation:

Version Three: Abigail scanned several items: a box of corn-flakes, a can of peas, two cartons of eggs. Bleach. Fish. Apples. With every pass of her hand, the scanner made a sound like a heart hooked to a machine.

Notice how the syntax changes the rhythm of the passage. The long opening sentence followed by three one-word sentences creates a little dance of words. The final sentence begins with a prepositional phrase rather than the conventional subject-verb-object, and includes a simile that suggests something about the character's life. Does Abigail herself feel like a heart hooked to a machine? Already the story seems to promise a character's transition from one state to another. Varied sentence constructions, telling details, evocative images—these small descriptive choices help even the slimmest stories crackle with life.

If your stories are small and your style unadorned, take care to vary your construction and include a relevant image every so often. The life of your story depends on it.

A CASE FOR MAXIMALISM

"Maximalism" is not a literary term, exactly. John Barth used it to describe large, sweeping novels that present entire worlds, such as Pynchon's *Gravity's Rainbow*. Nowadays the term accurately describes the backlash against minimalism. Suddenly, editors are receiving truckloads of stories that would delight a Victorian: elaborate settings, lush descriptions, event piled upon event, casts of thousands. Loquacious narrators are telling the stories of their lives and including everybody else's stories while they're at it. Many of these stories are wonderfully literary, beguiling, and hugely entertaining. Before you rush to pad your stories with outtakes, however, remember that although less isn't always more, *more* isn't always more, either. Every word counts, whether the story is long and lush or short and spare. Take that detour if you must, but make sure it winds back to the main road.

You could "maximalize" the story about Abigail the grocery clerk by exploring some past events or people from her life: A rock concert at which she met a roadie who gave her drugs and broke her heart; her father's last day at home before he left with another woman; a teacher who changed her grade after she pretended to cry. These detours—lengthy and complicated as they may be—make sense because they relate to Abigail's present-day story, which involves a man who claims to be auditioning women for a movie. He's probably lying, but Abigail can't afford not to believe him. The remembered events (rock concert; Dad's last day; grade change) are important because they remind her of her acting ability (crying for the teacher), and of men who lie (Dad and the roadie).

One way to manage a "maximal" story is to keep a *strong stylistic focus*. The prose style focuses the story. In her novel *The Shipping News*, E. Annie Proulx focuses an episodic story about a newsman in Newfoundland by using deliberately eccentric prose. Peppered with the foreign-sounding vocabulary of Newfoundland, the prose style reminds us at all times that the main character is a stranger in a strange land. Also, Proulx often begins sentences with the verb rather than the subject, giving her prose the clipped, imperative feel of newspaper headlines, a stylistic quirk that keeps the newsman central to our experience.

Perhaps we could find a similar stylistic focus in our story about Abigail the grocery clerk. Perhaps Abigail is remembering incidents from her life—the roadie, her father, and the teacher—as if they had occurred in a movie she once saw. Why not incorporate movie-style language into the prose? The first digression could begin like this:

> The last time she had taken a man at his word was in May, on the day of the annular eclipse of the sun. She burst out the sliding doors at the end of her shift to find the day eerily still, the chatty spring birds gone silent. A shadow passed over the parking lot with the sepia tone of an old movie. Cut to evening. A rock concert in progress. Girl, late teens, appears at the door, waving the backstage passes she won by being the fifteenth caller. She is allowed in, only to find a thicket of roadies shielding the fleeing band.
>
> She: Your hair's too long.
>
> He: Who the hell are you?
>
> She: Your hair's too long. I can't see your eyes.
>
> He offers her a shot of tequila, and an unfiltered cigar-

ette, and some pretty pink pills she can never remember the name of.

She slid a pound of ground turkey over the scanner and winced at the sound. *Cut to present,* she thought grimly.

The other digression could have a similar movie-reel format. No matter how many times Abigail digresses from the present, the readers will not be left wondering what happened to the girl in the grocery store, because every stylistic flourish that suggests a movie will also suggest the present-action story about the movie maker. All the extra characters and story lines will be unified by style.

If Abigail's story is about something that doesn't lend itself to stylistic innovation, you might want to focus the narrative by using a *central image.* A house. A color. A pet. A dress. Let's say the story is about Abigail's being burdened by a family pattern of heroism. She works double shifts to support her mother and grandmother, lovely yet sickly women who are beyond reproach. People seem to think it should be a privilege for Abigail to waste her youth caring for them; all the women in the family, from Eve on down, have made selflessness their *raison d'être.* Abigail's great-great aunt once saved a hypothermic baby by ripping off the beaded skirt of her wedding dress and wrapping the child in it, scandalizing onlookers and saving the child. Abigail tells this story to one of her customers, then remembers another story, one about her grandmother:

> Of course, there was a war on. She rationed salt. She rationed sugar. She rationed butter. She rationed her deepest wants, waiting for her man—Abigail's grandfather—to come home. She had a dress in her closet, a soft cotton sheath with real brass buttons. She had Uncle Geoffrey take her picture and send it to Grampa in the Philippines. A beautiful blonde woman in a sky-blue dress.

The story goes on to tell about the progress of the war and the toll on the women back home. Shortages become crises, and the grandmother ends up cutting the brass buttons from the dress as a donation to the war effort. The dress is simply not the same dress now, so she remakes it into a bunting for the baby who will turn out to be Abigail's mother.

Then Abigail remembers a third dress story, this one involving her mother, who once hand-sewed an Easter dress and left it on the doorstep of an impoverished playmate of Abigail's. By this time Abigail is tired and cranky from what is becoming a thunderous noise from the grocery scanner. She tears off her smock—a tacky polyester thing with her name stitched in orange letters. She leaves work, goes straight to a store, and wastes a week's pay on a new dress, something tight and trashy, a dress that couldn't possibly become a prop in yet another story about selflessness. Abigail's story incorporates several generations of stories, and yet it feels unified because of the common detail of the dress.

Another way to focus an expansive narrative is to use a *strong setting*. George Eliot used a place—the fictitious Middlemarch—to weave many separate story lines in her novel of the same name. Alice Munro often uses place to unify her delightfully meandering stories. *Strong first-person narrators* can focus a story, too. Narrators with quirky observations and charming voices can wander far off the path with barely a whimper from the readers, who feel tethered to the story by way of the narrator's voice.

Unifying a narrative with any number of these stylistic strategies offers you a chance to expand your story's horizons while retaining the illusion that it is being told with exactly the right number of words.

AVOIDING SENTIMENTALITY AND MELODRAMA

One of the pitfalls of generous description is sentimentality and melodrama. The more you love your characters, the more you must watch out for overblown descriptions. Oh, how tempting it is to wring our damp hands when our beloved characters are suffering!

Our personal feelings about our characters' plights are directly related to the number of modifiers we use. Mr. Smith becomes "lonely old Mr. Smith"; a drowned mouse becomes a "poor little mouse"; a virtuous young boy becomes a "sincere young sprite with clear blue eyes." Consider the following description of a man reaching the summit of a mountain:

He wiped the beads of sweat from his feverish brow, hoisted himself over the last, excruciating outcropping, and gasped victoriously at the triumph of nature that lay before him in all its dewy beauty. A magnificent blue sky hung silently above him, velvety blue valleys lay below him, and all around him the snow-capped peaks gleamed in the sun. He sat down, exhausted and happy, as the sweet blue tundra flowers danced with vicarious joy.

All right, already! the readers cry. You want to *move* your readers, not steamroll them. Note the number of adjectives and adverbs here: "feverish"; "victoriously"; "last, excruciating"; "dewy"; "magnificent blue"; "silently"; and on and on. Over ten modifiers within three sentences. To compound the problem, the modifiers are ordinary words used in the ordinary way. Where are the surprises in this passage, the fresh turns of phrase? *Remedy Number One: Edit your adverbs, count your adjectives.*

Compounding the problem of too many modifiers is the use of cliché: "fevered brow"; "triumph of nature"; "blue valleys"; "snow-capped peaks." These hackneyed phrases add nothing new to the readers' perceptions and serve to make the prose embarrassingly sentimental. *Remedy Number Two: Avoid cliché.*

Next, note the use of the pathetic fallacy in the last line. Pathetic fallacy is a term that describes the bad habit of ascribing human emotions or qualities to nature or inanimate objects. Those tundra flowers can no more feel vicarious joy than they can fry an egg. Sometimes the pathetic fallacy *can* be used effectively:

The house was obscured by a fence of cruel spikes.

Or:

The orchard trees, bowed and halfhearted, had been twisted into submission by Mr. Abel's hacksaw.

Images like these can work as metaphors in the appropriate story. But when you resort to grateful daisies or happy hydrangeas you've probably crossed the line. *Remedy Number Three: Avoid the pathetic fallacy.*

WRAP-UP

A writer's style is not immutable; style often changes to suit a given story. Although certain writers can be said to have a "practical" style and others a "lyrical" style, individual novels and stories by the same writer will demonstrate his or her so-called style to varying degrees. Even the most famous stylists vary their prose depending on the story at hand. Certain stories by James Joyce are more "Joycean" than others, for example. Ann Beattie is more "Beattian" in *Falling in Place* than she is in *Picturing Will.* Style evolves as much from the creation as it does from the creator.

Sometimes descriptive style matches the content of a story, and sometimes style and content contrast. Either way, the descriptive style can enrich the story you want to tell. Plain prose and simple constructions may reinforce the theme of simplicity you want in a story about a cloistered nun; a more lyrical style, on the other hand, may suggest the complexity of the nun's inner life. Wait until you have a few drafts on paper before you make a final decision. Style evolves over the course of many drafts, and you should allow it to change as you come to know your characters better.

Certain descriptive styles come in and out of vogue, and it's hard to resist their pull. Minimalism, which came into fashion during the seventies with the stories of Raymond Carver, made a big splash and was copiously imitated. Poorly executed minimalist stories have a dull, monochromatic feel that comes from a style that is intended to be simple but comes out simply flat. Minimalism requires exquisite telling detail and an inherently interesting situation.

As a backlash against the ubiquitous minimalism, stories are now getting bigger, sprawlier, and more lushly described. Big, multi-parted stories require stylistic unity in order to feel whole. A strong stylistic focus, a central image, a strong setting, or an unusual first-person narrator are stylistic techniques that can help you shape an overgrown story.

Maximalism, like minimalism, is a trend. Fiction fashions come and go, and the only way to survive these waves is to ignore them. Write your stories however they demand to be written—in vogue or out.

One descriptive style that is never in vogue, however, is sentimentality and melodrama. You can avoid this snakepit by scrupulously editing your prose. Measure your modifiers to avoid overwriting; weed out all clichés; and never commit the pathetic fallacy, which is ascribing human emotions to natural phenomena or inanimate objects.

Descriptive style profoundly shapes your readers' experience. Style is not a set of authorial quirks! It is a set of deliberate decisions, made over a series of drafts, that becomes an integral part of the story's impact.

CHAPTER 7

DESCRIPTION AND SETTING

DESCRIPTION OF SETTING is probably what Elmore Leonard meant when he said (possibly apocryphally), "I try not to write the parts people skip." It is true that pages-long accounts of the vineyards of France or the houses of San Francisco or the mustard fields of Virginia or the streets of Greenwich Village have the dangerous potential to put readers to sleep, but only if the description seems like an after-thought, or a writer's self-indulgence. When you take care to make a description of setting integral to the story—that is, if it sets a tone or mood, foreshadows future events, or suggests the characters' motives or desires—then you will be able to keep your readers engaged.

DETAILS THAT TELL A STORY

If Edith Wharton had set *Ethan Frome* in the Deep South instead of New England, she would have been compelled to write a different book. The lugubrious heat of southern Mississippi could not rein-force the frigidity of her characters' loveless existence—Wharton needed the brittle winter landscape of Vermont to fulfill her novel's purpose. Setting is as important to certain stories as the characters who inhabit that setting. Can you imagine *The Great Gatsby* set in Minneapolis, or *Oliver Twist* set on a farm in southern Italy?

Not all stories require a strong sense of place. Many successful novels and stories take place in nameless cities or anonymous yards or on unidentifiable stretches of road. Their energy and atmosphere come not from setting, but from the complexities of character, the intricacies of plot, the quality of language. If setting *is* part of a story, however, it should have a function other than to create atmosphere or background. Descriptions of place are like snapshots—they record a setting. Unfortunately, some snapshots, like some descriptions, are more involving than others.

Imagine looking at your uncle Simon's photographs of his trip to Wyoming. You sift through view after view of dark mountain ranges, cloud-filled sky, red sunsets, and long shots of prairie dogs, trying to keep your eyes open. Why does magnificence always seem so dull in reproduction? Probably because most people aren't good photographers: they snap their cameras with no eye for composition. Nothing stands out. Still, you come upon a happy accident occasionally: a moment before Uncle Simon snapped Mount Rushmore, his hat blew off his head and began rolling end over end into the middle of his shot. The result is a picture of Uncle Simon's fishing cap floating like an offering before the stony likenesses of four American presidents. Not only do you suddenly have an image you can remember, you have a way of understanding why Uncle Simon was so awed by his trip, and you know what he means when he tells you, "I felt small."

Descriptions of setting should provide that same click of understanding. You can go on for pages about the white cliffs of Dover, but until you throw in the equivalent of Uncle Simon's fishing cap, the yawning readers are reading (or, more likely, skipping) the equivalent of a dimestore postcard. The purpose of place description is not to provide a general background or atmosphere, but a *specific* background or atmosphere. Telling the readers that the sunset is beautiful or that the town was built in 1723 is fine; but if the sunset turns out to be the last thing the character sees in the living world, and 1723 is the birthdate of the character's earliest known ancestor, then the setting takes on added weight.

Every description of place should have a memorable quality that hints at the story's meaning. Otherwise, you're just filling up space. Let's take as an example a story about a woman visiting Quebec City, Canada:

Version One: Maxine walked along the Dufferin Terrace, a walled promenade that surrounded the upper part of Quebec

City. The sky above her was a lovely blue, and below her the St.
Lawrence River ruffled along, busy with boats. As she ap-
proached the end of the Terrace, she could see the Chateau
Frontenac, its turrets gleaming in the afternoon light.

This description is not bad, but neither is it breathtaking or even
useful. Nothing in it gives the slightest clue as to the reason for Maxine's presence in this city. The turrets are nice, and the "ruffling"
river is mildly interesting, but the description is too generic to allow
the readers to "see" the city in any particular way.

Benign descriptions of setting add nothing to a story's purpose.
If the setting is static and perfunctory, existing only as an introduction
to other events, then it serves merely as a way into the story, and that's
not good enough. In the example of Maxine in Quebec, you should
give your readers some small indication about what the setting means
to her. Is it intimidating? liberating? scary? exciting? Maxine could
be local, a tourist, a travel guide on her lunch hour, or a thief on the
lam. Right now she isn't much more than another landmark in the
setting.

Let's try this description again, with an eye toward giving place
description a purpose:

> **Version Two:** Maxine walked along the Dufferin Terrace,
> practicing her French. She whispered the words for *please* and
> *thank you* and *how much*, occasionally glancing over the wall at the
> cliff's dizzying drop into the blue-black water of the St. Lawrence
> River. A half-mile ahead of her the Chateau Frontenac already
> appeared to loom—frothy and ridiculous against the modest
> jumble of buildings that surrounded it. She stopped to stare,
> trying to pick out her room from the hundreds of tiny curtained
> windows. Slices of sky appeared through the hotel's dozens of
> turrets, making greener the ancient hotel's rusting copper roof-
> tops.

This revised description gives your readers a much stronger sense of
a woman in a foreign place. The walk on the terrace takes place in
the context of her practicing her French, which immediately sets her
up as a stranger. The proximity of the cliff lends a mild sense of
danger or disequilibrium to her experience. The "hundreds of tiny,

curtained windows" suggest the hotel's enormity, but also suggests the anonymity Maxine must feel as she looks for her room. At the same time, the great chateau looks "frothy and ridiculous," rather than imposing or intimidating. Maxine may be alone in a large and foreign place, but the whimsical description of the hotel suggests that she is not frightened at the prospect. These details are the equivalent of Uncle Simon's fishing hat, for they place Maxine in Quebec City in a way that allows us to "see" both her and the city.

Relative Details

Besides making the story itself more evident, the revised version improves on the original in another way. The various parts of the setting—the sky, the hotel, the terrace—are rendered in relationship to each other.

One way to make a setting come alive is to describe one thing in relationship to something else. The size of a tree becomes more vivid if you describe the bird's nest wedged into the end of one of the branches, or the nuthatch working its way down miles of trunk. A river can look black against a blue sky, or blue against a backdrop of pale buildings.

In Version One of the above description, each detail is independent of every other detail. First we see the terrace, then the river, then the chateau. We don't know how big one thing is compared to another, or how far apart the things are, how impressive they are to Maxine, or even what anything actually looks like, except that the chateau has turrets. In Version Two, however, the chateau becomes a focal point because of its contrast with the "modest jumble of buildings" that surrounds it. We assume that the chateau must then be "immodest" and that it stands apart from or above the "jumble." We "see" the city through that one contrasting detail, and understand why the chateau "already seems to loom" when Maxine is a half mile away. Similarly, the sky is not simply a sky, but a detail that visually shapes and colors the rusted copper rooftops of the chateau. Relating details to each other in this way adds depth and accuracy to a setting, inviting readers into the world of the story.

Sensory Details

As in any good description, sensory details can help shape the read-ers' experience. Consider the following descriptions of the same pond:

> **Version One:** Belle turned off Lucas Street to where the gravel path wound around the pond. The sky was blue, the day warm, the ground solid under her feet. She walked down the path to where the reeds began, and looked across the water to where some water lilies floated over the brackish surface. A fam-ily of ducks made their way through the lilies, quacking softly. A wind disturbed the water, and she closed her eyes. She loved this place; she could get away from her family here. It was peace-ful and calm.

> **Version Two:** Belle held to the path until it crooked around the south end of the pond. She stopped for a few moments simply to listen, then followed the trail she had matted into the grass over the past two weeks. It wound through the reeds and ended at the edge of the water. She sat down, pressing her hands into the spongy earth, listening hard, dissecting the confusion of sound: an oriole's mournful piping, the rustle of grass, the white noise of insects, the slap of muskrats diving from the banks, the intimate quavering of mallards steering through snags of water lily. By now she could identify each note of the pond's great teeming. Behind her, on the other side of the trees, whined the morning commute on Lucas Street, high and insistent and inescapable. Farther still, she could (she imag-ined) hear the clash of words—ugly, staccato, incomprehensi-ble—in the cluttered kitchen she had come here to escape.
>
> A gust of wind moved the water, making the world reflected there—tree, cloud, sky—seem to explode, then calmly reassem-ble itself. She looked to the far bank. A blot of yellow moved through the brushy tangle of the pond's far side, a warbler look-ing for nesting material. It was the time of year for making homes.

Version One introduces any old character looking at any old pond. Version Two introduces a troubled woman coming to a unique place that she has chosen for its restorative qualities. What's the difference? Look at the sensory quality of the detail. In Version Two, Belle is taking in this place very specifically, through her senses. The generic description of the first version—reeds, ducks, and water lilies—gives way in the second version to more specific detail (the sound of orioles, mallards, muskrats) and the occasional visual surprise, like "blots of yellow [moving] through the brushy tangle."

Notice, too, that in Version One the details are almost exclusively visual, and in Version Two the details are almost exclusively aural. Describing the pond through sound rather than sight works in two ways. One, sound makes the pond much more sensually alive, more a real place than a snapshot in which "the sky was blue, the day warm." When we experience a place, we often tune in through sound as much as sight. Here, we "see" everything even more clearly through the vehicle of sound, because sound connotes movement: the mallards' quavering brings to mind a raft of birds moving over the water; the insects' "white noise" brings to mind harmless swarms of nearly invisible bugs; the sound of the muskrats brings to mind their disappearing backs and dripping tails; even the "whine of traffic" conjures images of incessantly moving cars.

The focus on sound suggests that Belle can dissect the "confusion of sound" in the pond in a way she cannot dissect the "incomprehensible" sounds in the "cluttered kitchen she had come here to escape." The pond is not simply fill-in or background or atmosphere: Belle's presence there is purposeful and gives us information about her. Every noise and color in that pond has a counterpoint in the house that Belle is escaping. Even as she marvels at the "intimate quavering of the mallards," she can hear the "whine of traffic just over the ridge of trees, high and insistent and inescapable." The conflict in the story is beginning to suggest itself through the description of place.

It's easy to get lost in the beauty of your own prose when describing setting, but you can't afford to forget for one moment that you are *writing a story*. Every beat of the prose must have some bearing on the story you wish to reveal.

THE SETTING'S HISTORY

Another way to reinforce conflict in a story is to use the historical significance of certain settings. Suppose you decide to set a story in

Boston's North End. You know the area well, and you believe its rich history will add interest and atmosphere to a story about a brother and sister. You're right—the setting does have potential, as long as you include its history in a way that naturally fits the story. Avoid presenting historical details for their own sake:

> Tom snaked his way through the winding streets of Boston's North End, his throat constricting with the news he had yet to deliver. He couldn't remember where Audrey lived; perhaps if he kept driving something would begin to look familiar. He made another turn. The tidy buildings—vestiges of a Puritan vision that began in 1630 with John Winthrop—gave the now prosperous state capital the look of a little village.

The history here detracts from your story. Just as your readers begin to wonder about the news Tom has to deliver, you subject them to a travel-book aside about Colonial America. It feels like an interruption. What if you used the history to magnify something that's going on inside the character?

> Tom snaked his way through the winding streets of Boston's North End, his throat constricting with undelivered news. He leaned against the steering wheel, peering around and through the tidy Colonial buildings, searching for a landmark. He knew only that she lived near the Old North Church, where Paul Revere had once ridden frantically over these same crooked streets, sounding the alarm.

Here, Paul Revere's "frantic" ride gives an outer shape to Tom's inner turmoil. By evoking Paul Revere's famous ride, you imply that the news Tom has yet to deliver is bad, or at least calamitous in some way. We also get the feeling that Tom would like to be able to shout out his news the way Paul Revere did, but his constricted throat shows us that for some reason he can't. History works beautifully here, giving us not only an interesting glimpse of historical Boston, but an insightful glimpse into the main character.

A historical setting can reinforce a story by illuminating theme, revealing character, enriching plot. A famous battlefield might enrich a story about a cutthroat business deal or a cracking marriage; the town of Bethlehem could add humor or pathos to a story about a carpenter's wife on her first bus tour. If you choose a setting that readers readily recognize as a historical landmark, you have more or less obligated yourself to use the history of that place to illuminate parts of your story.

SETTINGS LARGE AND SMALL

Some descriptions of setting are big and sweeping, some minute and compact. You have to decide which kind works best for a particular story. Do you need the whole forest, or just one tree? In a story about a young boy feeling dwarfed by his boisterous family, the mountain setting should probably be large:

> He lay in his bed, staring out at the malevolent sweep of mountain that ringed the valley.

If the boy feels strong and powerful, the same setting might take on a more accessible quality:

> From here he imagined he could make out the starry shapes of wild azaleas that blazed along the slope.

Almost any large setting can be made small—that is, readily accessible to the readers—if you attend to detail. The pebbly shingles of the town's black roofs. The green bottle floating in the middle of the ocean. The *Bloomingdale's* bag tangled in a Central Park tree. With these details, you guide the readers' eyes to the specific and away from the general landscape.

PROBLEMS WITH "ACTUAL" PLACES

When my first novel, *Secret Language*, came out early in 1993, I was asked by a local deejay to come in for a radio interview. The novel is set in Portland, Maine, where I live, and contains occasional references to streets and landmarks in the city. One of the first questions the disc jockey (who had read and liked the book) asked was this: "About your main character, Faith—is her house the one at the end of Norwood Street?" When I told him that Faith's house existed only in my imagination, he seemed disappointed, for he was sure he had located exactly the house in the novel. Everything fit, he insisted: the shape of the lawn, the bird feeders hanging from the trees, the porch and walk. Of course I was pleased that my invented place seemed so real to him, but I was also bemused by the problem of putting fictional people in real places.

Beware the Locals

One problem with describing a setting that is real is that reality changes. In the interest of authenticity, you might move to Seattle for a year and write an entire novel there, meticulously recording street names and architectural styles and common surnames and typical weather. By the time the book appears two or three (or ten) years later, however, the Good Times Deli on Washington Street has been torn down and turned into Tom's Texaco. Carver Avenue, the scene of a head-on collision that begins Part II of the book, is now a one-way street. There is no overestimating the glee some readers experience when coming upon geographical glitches in their home turf. "Your book was wonderful," they write. "However, there are no middle schools in Greenfield. We go from elementary to junior high." Your admirable impulse to create accurate descriptions has blindsided you by delivering exactly the opposite effect you intended. Instead of wowing your readers with accuracy, you've made them fretful and petty.

Fictionalizing Reality

Why not fictionalize an actual setting? You can make up a neighborhood and place it "near" a familiar landmark:

> Vernon's house on Drake Street was a ten-minute walk from Harvard University. The proximity of that famous institution was evident in Vernon's neighborhood only by the occasional plastic bag from the Harvard Coop that got caught in the stiff tentacles of the naked, spindly trees or mashed into soggy, unrecognizable lumps between the sidewalks' yawning cracks.

Notice that the neighborhood is meticulously described with no mention of its exact location. (Be sure to check a map to make sure there is no "real" Drake Street anywhere near Harvard.) Your readers don't know whether the Drake Street neighborhood is ten minutes north, south, east, or west of Harvard; they understand that even though Harvard exists in real life, you are making up the rest of the map. They may even assume that the fictional neighborhood is based on an area they know, but because the street names aren't real, they can't check your facts against a city map. The familiar landmark lends authenticity to your setting, but the rest of the place is yours to do with as you wish.

You can do this in reverse, too: fictionalize the landmark but make everything else accurate. This technique is useful if the landmark in question—a university, a museum, a church, a branch of government—is going to be used in the story. The main character might be the college chancellor, for example, or the pastor of the church, or the curator of the museum. To avoid dragging actual persons into your fiction, you might try something like the following:

> From her top-floor apartment on Morning Street, she could see all the way down Munjoy Hill, a ziggurat of rooftops that ended with the commanding spire of St. Mary's rising from the foot of the hill into the bleak winter sky.

This setting is familiar to anyone who lives in Portland, Maine, except that the church at the foot of Munjoy Hill is not "St. Mary's," it is the Cathedral of the Immaculate Conception. Why bother to change the name? Let's assume this is the beginning of a story that involves characters who work in and around the church and school. You certainly don't want to confuse actual persons—the president of the parish council, for example—with fictional characters. And you don't want people chiding you for getting the number of windows wrong, or putting the altar at the wrong end of the church, or abolishing the 10 a.m. mass for one that begins at 9:30. The solution is to fictionalize a local landmark simply by changing its name. By doing so, you make a pact with your readers: *I'm borrowing the church for a little while, okay?* Readers are more than happy to make the loan, and if you're lucky, the fictionalized landmark will become as real to them as the actual one.

WRAP-UP

Long descriptions of setting that function merely as backdrop or atmosphere can quickly wear a reader's patience. When describing the city or vacant lot or mountain range or fire escape that serves as your story's setting, keep in mind, always, that you are telling a story. How does this particular setting bear on the characters' actions? How do the characters perceive this setting? Does anything about this setting—its colors or odors or sounds—suggest the characters' inner conflicts and desires? The story's setting should be an integral part of the story you wish to tell.

Settings shouldn't be "the parts people skip." You must add details that remind readers that the setting has a purpose. An abandoned fishing line at the shore of a river, a pile of books on the library floor, a badminton net tangled on the church spire—these details keep the readers aware that a story is being unmasked even as it is being "set."

To get the most out of a description of setting, make the details relative to each other rather than important only to themselves. A thatched hut is made small by a description of the giant palm trees that shelter it; a crumbling brick sidewalk is made luminous by a description of the sun's path over its chipped surface. Remember, too, to engage all the senses: a place can be "seen" through sound and scent and touch and taste.

Sometimes the history of a place can be used to the story's advantage. An orphanage restored into a hotel might make a good setting for a story about a couple on vacation, hoping to get pregnant. A construction site might enhance a story about a friendship in need of repair.

Descriptions of setting can be majestic or modest, depending on the story's needs. The broad view—the vast rippled surface of a lake—can bring grandeur to your setting, and the specific details—the silvery eye of a fish—can bring to your setting a cozy smallness.

Real places present special description problems. A place you describe today with dogged accuracy may have been razed by the time your book or story gets into print. Also, when you try too hard to be accurate you risk the fretful reader's complaint that getting from Main to Broad requires two left turns, not three. On the other hand, real places lend authenticity to stories. You might experiment a little with blending fact and fiction. For example, you might set a story in a real city, then make up a neighborhood within that city. Or, you might use the actual neighborhood of that city, then change the name of the church or school or monument that defines it. Readers are very forgiving as long as they recognize the rules.

Setting can be as important to a story as character or plot, and requires as much descriptive attention as any other element of fiction. Give it the care it deserves—your reward will be a story that feels authentic and unified.

CHAPTER 8

SPECIAL DESCRIPTION PROBLEMS

No MATTER HOW GOOD OUR WRITING BECOMES, certain description problems are bound to crop up again and again. How do we describe an animal without making it seem like an illustration in a Peterson guide, or, even worse, a character in a Disney movie? How do we describe weather without resorting to cliché? How do we make a reader "hear" sound? The following strategies may help you solve these reoccurring problems of description.

DESCRIBING ANIMALS

If you include animals in your stories you are probably an animal lover. If you are an animal lover you probably share quarters with the world's smartest dog, the world's prettiest cat, or the world's most talented parakeet. Perhaps you talk to your animals as if they understand you. And, who knows, maybe they do. Please remember, though, that what works in life doesn't always work in fiction. Your eight-year-old Siamese might fetch your slippers, but a reader might not believe this of a fictional cat. So, as you are booting up your computer or sharpening your pencil or looking for your lucky pen, remind yourself that animals are not furry people, no matter how much you adore yours.

That said, how do you handle animals once you decide they do belong in your story? Like human characters, animals deserve to be rendered accurately, interestingly, and truthfully. If you err too much on the furry-person side, your animals end up looking like

Cinderella's sidekicks; too much on the field-guide side, your animals look like something mounted in a taxidermist's window.

Describing animals accurately is difficult, because all individual animals of a species, with few exceptions, look exactly the same. It is difficult to tell squirrels apart, for example, or rose-breasted gros-beaks, or caribou, or grizzly bears. Therefore, if you describe an animal accurately you offer a perfectly serviceable picture of a certain species of animal:

> Lisa's Saint Bernard followed her into the living room. It had a huge rounded head, a massive body, and loose jowls. "Sit, Chuckles," Lisa demanded, and the dog obeyed.

What you don't offer, however, is a picture of any *particular* animal of that species. Like human characters, each animal, closely observed, is unique:

> Lisa walked into the living room, her Saint Bernard lumbering behind her. It moved like a stevedore, barrel-chested and full of purpose. "Sit, Chuckles," Lisa demanded, and the dog obeyed, its wide and mournful face listing downward.

Here, you describe the dog as a Saint Bernard like any other—don't they all have mournful faces and barrel chests?—and yet you suggest the uniqueness of this particular animal through muscular verbs ("lumbering") and good use of simile ("like a stevedore") and intimations of personality ("full of purpose") that don't go so far as to make the animal a furry person. The vivid presentation has an added bonus: the name "Chuckles" is quite funny when applied to this serious, "mournful" creature.

Descriptions like this can so easily go wrong, of course. Language must be precise. Replacing a phrase like "his mournful face listing downward" with "he hung his head sadly" would violate the dog's animalness. In the first phrase, you are merely observing what the dog looks like, and in the second you are attributing emotion to a dog. Attributing human characteristics, emotions, or motivations to animals is called *anthropomorphism*—a major culprit in sentimental writing. The phrase "full of purpose" flirts with anthropomorphism, but it doesn't cross the line because it describes the dog's way of moving, not his moral integrity. Only if the passage were stuffed with other, similar phrases (describing, say, the dog's loyalty or bewilderment or fear or guilt) would the phrase "full of purpose" feel sentimental or corny.

My favorite animal description of all time is from Ralph Lombreglia's story "One-Woman Blues Revival":

> It was a mammoth raccoon on the windowsill, looking at her with his broad masked face. He was moving his pointy nose all around, smelling the pantry smells. His long, black claws hung over the edge of the sill.
>
> You couldn't live in Vermont without seeing lots of raccoons, but she'd never seen one this close up, so trusting and calm. She felt, after all these unsatisfactory years of adulthood, that she might finally be in a fairy tale. "Who the hell are you?" she said. "Do you talk?" To her great disappointment, he did not.

In this delightful passage, Lombreglia weds Disney to Peterson. The raccoon has a fanciful, cartoonish demeanor, "moving his pointy nose all around, smelling the pantry smells," but the description is accurate: "broad, masked face"; "long, black claws." Raccoons, perhaps more than any other animal, make fools of humans, because they're so darned cute we want to turn them into friends. Lombreglia acknowledges this impulse by revealing the woman's hope that "she might finally be in a fairy tale." He then yanks away any potential for sentimentality by having her ask, "Who the hell are you?" instead of saying something gluey like "Why, hello, little fellow." It's a brilliant passage because it acknowledges all our projections and (understandable) silliness about animals while reminding us that a raccoon is nothing more than, well, a raccoon.

Even if you stick to the most basic animal descriptions, you can jazz up the prose by paying attention to shades of color, thicknesses of coat, shapes of tails or paws or snouts. Consider different words for common features, or fresh similes that describe those features. A spotted leopard becomes a dappled cat. The shell of a tortoise might remind you of the sun-leathered surface of your grandfather's hands. The tail of a dog can resemble a hose or a bottle brush or an ostrich feather. You can make your animal characters seem unique or intelligent or charming or menacing by celebrating the very features and qualities that make them animals.

DESCRIBING WEATHER

Weather is part of our experience as human beings in this world, and references to weather are as impossible to avoid in literature as they are in casual conversation. Our awareness of weather is not awfully precise, however, unless we are barricading against a hurricane or shoveling out from a two-foot snowfall. The daily pleasantries we utter to each other—"Nice day, isn't it?"; "Think it'll rain?"; "Cold enough for you?"—are not really as much about weather as they are about our desire to connect with one another in a safe and superficial way. Safe and superficial is great for casual human relationships but deadly in fiction. Your literary descriptions of weather should be fresh and necessary rather than banal and irrelevant.

Direct and Indirect Description of Weather

Most readers like to know what the weather is like in a story they're reading—nothing elaborate, just a quick glimpse to determine whether it's winter or summer, raining or snowing. If you are using weather only to inform the readers—that is, if the weather actually has nothing to do with the events of the story—then your best bet is to keep the description as simple as possible:

> It had been raining for three days.

Or:

> When Tuesday finally came, the weather was clear and cold.

Or:

> By the time Harold reached his aunt's house, it was snowing.

These examples provide a quick scan, the literary equivalent of sticking your finger into the wind or your head out the window. By providing direct, literal description, you allow readers to take note of the weather and get on with the story. However, if the weather is going to have some effect on the events of the story or provide a certain kind of atmosphere that the story requires, you should try to make your account of the weather more memorable.

One way to do that is to describe the weather indirectly, by closely observing how certain kinds of weather make the world look. For example, instead of describing a day as frigid, you might have a character observe a frozen field. In Jack Holland's "The Yard," a story about a man remembering his boyhood experience of his grandfather's death, the raw and dreary day is revealed to us through the character's physical surroundings:

> The rain was standing in puddles between the cobblestones and in shallow little pools on the tops of the big barrels that were marshaled against the wall near the horse trough, row upon row, like great, dumpy soldiers. The puddles rippled in the cold February wind, which drove before it the little bits of straw floating on the stale water. The carts were covered with tarpaulin, their shafts lowered. My heart ached.

Note how little time the author spends on a direct account of the weather. He uses the words "rain" and "cold . . . wind," and that's it. Everything else is a *reflection* of the weather, from the "shallow . . . pools . . . on the barrels" to the "rippled" puddles to the "floating" straw to the carts "covered in tarpaulin." We get the impression of a very, very wet day after an extremely heavy rain, for water is everywhere. We can also imagine a grey sky, a bone-chilling cold, and a general dreariness, though the author does not describe these things directly.

Indirect description has two benefits. One, it delivers you from resorting to tired descriptions: rainy days, heavy snows, blue skies. Two, indirectness does three jobs at once. In the story excerpt above, the carefully observed reflections of weather give us the condition of the weather (rainy), the condition of the setting (a simple Irish village), and the condition of the observer (heartbroken). Here, the weather becomes a poignant reflection of a young boy's bewilderment and sorrow.

Engaging the Senses when Describing Weather

Weather is one of the most satisfying subjects for engaging all the senses. Weather can be *seen*, as in hailstones or snowflakes; weather can be *heard*, as in the drumming of rain on a tin roof; weather can be *felt* as moisture or heat or cold; weather can even be *tasted*, as in the sulphur tang of a steel mill on very hot days; and weather can be *smelled*, as in the scent of earth that comes with the first warm days after winter. Your senses give you a myriad of new ways to describe the familiar. Each sense describes a different aspect of the same weather.

Let's take a hot summer night and render it through all five senses:

Sight: Defeated and exhausted, Alice and I watched the August steam rising from the sidewalks.

Sound: We sat on the back porch, the hot night punctuated only by the click of ice in our glasses and the occasional snap of the neighbor's screen door.

Touch: The air was so thick on my arms it felt like sleeves.

Taste: My first sip of mint julep on Emma's steamy veranda meant summer was here at last.

Smell: The night was so hot and clear I could smell the lilacs from Jack's garden a half mile down the road.

Notice how the use of the senses transforms weather from reportage to experience. If your story depends on weather for a certain kind of atmosphere or insight into the characters' situation, then it is not enough to merely *report* the weather; it is your obligation to *evoke* the weather. The sensory details in the preceding examples turn weather into part of the story rather than a mere backdrop. Steam rising from the sidewalks makes the characters' defeat even more unbearable. The sound of ice in glasses and screen doors banging evoke all of summer, not just one hot night. The feeling of air as "sleeves" puts us, quite literally (and uncomfortably), inside the character's skin. The taste of mint julep evokes a certain lifestyle as well as the advent of summer. The scent of lilacs infuses the story with a small-town neighborliness.

When describing weather, try to forget about the exact condition of the weather and instead explore the ways in which certain weather makes the world look and smell and feel.

DESCRIBING EMOTION

Because some writers fear being seen as melodramatic or sentimental, they avoid emotion-filled passages in their writing. Their characters can't afford to be deliriously happy or ferociously angry or desperately sad; they move through an emotionally neutral narrative in which their inner state is merely hinted at. The steel-gray sky serves as a metaphor for despair; a snippet of dialogue reveals a well of pain; a muted action—stirring sugar into a cup of tea, or pruning a hedge—suggests anger, or loneliness, or joy. All of these techniques are useful, even admirable, but sometimes we can get so worried about being caught in the act of sentimentality that our fiction suffers an even worse fate: It becomes bloodless. After a while the readers begin to cry out for a character to, well, cry out.

How your characters cry out marks the difference between heartfelt prose and schlock. Take a character with a broken heart (please!)—how do you describe this all-too-common feeling? The heart in question can break, or ache, or constrict; the owner of the heart can weep or sigh or sob; he or she can verbally express heartbrokenness by saying "I'm heartbroken" or "I'm sad" or "I want to die." These descriptions are true enough, but they don't move us in any specific way. It's a challenge to convey common, cliché, yet very human emotions without sounding melodramatic. You know you're in trouble if the expression of emotion is all cerebral:

> She was heartbroken. Bill had left her and now she was all alone with her tears, her aching heart and her sorrowful memories of a happier time. She felt she would never smile again. "I want to die," she said aloud.

Okay, we know this is awful. Why? There is not one concrete image in the entire passage, that's why. It's all *thoughts*. The character sounds like a self-pitying blubberpuss instead of a woman who is genuinely and rightfully sad. By transforming her fuzzy thoughts into concrete images, you can turn melodrama into poignancy:

That night, lying in her damp sheets, she listened to her heart. Across the room his face stared out of the photograph that seemed already to be yellowing. She stared into the dark, imagining she could see dust gathering on the frame. He was gone.

In this revision you employ strong, accessible images to invite your readers into the character's world. Damp sheets, yellow photograph, dust—these things are real. We can see and feel them. They allow us to experience what the character experiences. We understand why her heart is broken because we can see her transformed room.

The following example works in the same way, by avoiding the cerebral and embracing the physical. A man is visiting his dying mother. They are on the back porch, watching the sunset:

He watched the last red strand of sky fade to dark. "That's that," his mother said. Then his heart broke.

Again, you give us specific images rather than thoughts or feelings. The direct information—"his heart broke"—comes only after we have been outside the character for a few beats. First we watch the end of the sunset, then we hear the mother's cryptic comment. Only then do you inform us that the character's heart is breaking. You *return* us to the character with a jolt, so that we recognize his sorrow at the same moment he does.

In the following two examples, the emotion is fortified not by an outside image, but by the *behavior* of the characters:

Sarah leaned against the trellis, stricken with longing.
Henry crossed his hands over his chest, first one and then the other. He held them there, protecting his heart.

The act of leaning against a trellis gives weight and credibility to the information that Sarah is filled with longing. The measured act of crossing his hands over his chest emphasizes Henry's fragile emotional state. Cerebral prose like "Sarah was filled with a sudden, indescribable longing" or "Henry was overcome with grief" cannot by itself tell the tale; you need the characters' bodies—their arms and fingers and eyelids and knees—to fully convey to the readers that the character is a human being who is suffering or savoring or fleeing or fuming. The difference between cerebral and physical prose is the difference between reading about an accident in the paper and pulling your own father from a crumpled car.

When managing emotional moments in your fiction, remember that the emotional moment itself—the sorrow, the joy, the shame, the rage—depends mightily on the prose that leads up to it. Overblown, melodramatic lead-ins only diminish the emotional moment. Conversely, stingy descriptions might leave readers ill-prepared for a dramatic emotional display. Strong, concrete images in place of abstract thought should carry the day.

The best build-up to an emotional moment I know of in recent fiction is in Kazuo Ishiguro's deeply affecting novel *The Remains of the Day*. The first-person narrator is Mr. Stevens, the aging butler of Darlington Hall, who embarks on a "motoring trip" during which he looks back on his life, trying to reassure himself that he has served humanity by serving a "great gentleman." His doubts about Lord Darlington's true nature—and therefore his own worth—slowly take shape as the narrative progresses. The final stop on his trip brings him face to face with Miss Kenton, who was once the housekeeper at Darlington Hall. Her crackling spirit was the one (unadmitted) bright spot in Stevens's life, until his excessive reserve drove her away. They meet. They talk. And, finally, Miss Kenton confesses her feelings:

> "But that doesn't mean to say, of course, there aren't occasions now and then—extremely desolate occasions—when you think to yourself: 'What a terrible mistake I've made with my life.' And you get to thinking about a different life, a *better* life you might have had. For instance, I get to thinking about a life I may have had with you, Mr. Stevens. And I suppose that's when I get angry over some trivial little thing and leave. But each time I do so, I realize before long—my rightful place is with my husband. After all, there's no turning back the clock now. One can't be forever dwelling on what might have been. One should realize one has as good as most, perhaps better, and be grateful."

I do not think I responded immediately, for it took me a moment or two to fully digest these words of Miss Kenton. Moreover, as you might appreciate, their implications were such as to provoke a certain degree of sorrow within me. Indeed—

why should I not admit it?—at that moment, my heart was breaking.

From a man whose life has been dedicated to submerging his emotions, the simple words "my heart was breaking" are enough to break our own hearts. We understand that the entire book has been a preparation for Mr. Stevens's ordinary human admission. The hapless aside—"why should I not admit it?"—makes his admission all the more poignant, for had he been able to admit such things twenty years ago, he would be telling a different story now. Straight-laced words like "moreover" and "implications" only heighten the emotional impact by contrasting his proper outside with his disheveled inside. What an unforgettable moment!

Good fiction is about human interaction, and human interaction takes place in the realm of emotion. Let your characters' hearts break, let their laughter ripple, let their shame consume them. Beware the critics, though. Several years ago a certain old, well-regarded magazine ran a short story by a certain young, well-regarded writer. The story was about a former child movie star, now an old man, who visits a dying little girl in the hospital. Granted, the story's premise is a minefield for a writer wanting to avoid sentimentality and melodrama, but this particular writer's gorgeous prose rescued the problematic premise; the story became a brief, moving account of a moment between a man with his best years behind him and a child with her best years never to come. Still, this story was listed in another magazine as the "worst short story of the year."

No matter how you decide to depict emotion in your fiction, you run the risk of a bloodless critic looking down the long slope of his nose and pronouncing your story a bowl of mush. Take the risk.

DESCRIBING SOUND

At various points in this book we have discussed the virtue of "engaging the senses" in fiction, including the sense of sound. The aural aspects of description can be the most compelling and inviting to readers, and yet many writers overlook sound, probably because it can be so difficult to convey accurately. Sure, we can write of the "splash" of water or the "rustle" of leaves or the "roll" of thunder or the "squish" of mud; these sound-words are familiar to readers, easily heard. It's the subtler sounds—a cat walking over gravel, a basketball banking off the backboard—that challenge our powers of description. Can we duplicate those sounds without writing gibberish?

Well, sure. We can even make up words if we have to. Get up and go to the nearest door. Open it and close it a few times. What does the door moving back and forth over the carpet *really* sound like? The sound is probably something like a *huff* or a *shuff* or a *hoof* or a *thuff*. If you're in a cavernous room with no rugs, the sound might be brighter and sharper: *clack* or *crick* or *crock* or *quick*. Are all these words suitable for describing the sound your character hears when his sister-in-law enters his study? Probably not. It depends on the prose that precedes the sound.

If you've written this story in straightforward, traditional prose, then a made-up word to describe a sound might feel false. For example:

> Lyndon leaned over his papers, staring out the window into the dark. He worried about Annabelle. She didn't trust him; he could see it in the narrow blue eyes, the suspicious curl of her lips whenever she condescended to speak to him. He spread his hands over the papers, protecting them. Then he heard her step in the hall, and the shuff of the door as she pushed it open.

In this passage the word "shuff" is at best puzzling and at worst confusing. The prose is too straight-laced (which is not to say bad) to support the sudden entrance of a made-up word. But what if the sound of the door is important to the scene? Perhaps you could find a more conventional word:

> . . . She didn't trust him; he could see it in the narrow blue eyes, the suspicious curl of her lips whenever she condescended to speak to him. He spread his hands over the papers, protecting them. Then he heard her step in the hall, and the door whispering open.

In revision the sound of the door opening is a "whispering," which is a conventional, accessible sound-word that describes not only the opening door (probably swinging open over a carpet) but the general unease of the main character, who is deep in thought, and worried. The "whisper" is perfect, the "shuff" distracting.

What if you were to write the same passage in more inventive, imagistic prose? Now the word *shuff* feels natural:

> Lyndon leaned over his papers. Night covered the open windows like a grainy cloth: impenetrable, opaque, vaguely dirty. He worried about Annabelle. She didn't trust him; he could see it in the hooded slits of her eyes, the suspicious slope of her lips whenever she condescended to speak to him. He spread his hands over the papers, protecting them. Then he heard her step in the hall, and the shuff of the door as she pushed it open.

In this version the prose leading up to the word *shuff* is plumped with simile ("like a grainy cloth") and various other images ("hooded slits," "slope of her lips," "impenetrable, opaque"), allowing the made-up word to stand unprotested. Although one style is no better than the other, each has its own intrinsic rules. You don't wear a tweed blazer with a chiffon dress, and you don't use words like *shuff* in conventional prose.

And what of those other, simpler sound-words—those splashes and rustles and squishes? Good prose includes familiar sounds: the crack of a bat, the flutter of wings, the roar of the wind, the shatter of glass. Horses neigh and nicker, cats yowl and mew, dogs bark and whine, birds twitter and cheep. Fires crackle, bombs explode, cars roar, houses creak. This is the way ordinary people describe the world, and there is nothing wrong with these ordinary sound-words. They belong in good prose, just as the ordinary but necessary verbs *to be* and *to have* belong there. You'll find great satisfaction, though, in periodically replacing these conventional sound-words with something a little more inventive, just as you sometimes replace familiar verbs. One entertaining way to transform sound is to literally mix up conventional sound associations. Horses neigh and houses creak— can these sounds work in reverse?

> Harriet lay in her great-grandmother's bed, exhausted. How many crates of knick-knacks and dishes and doilies had they packed today? Twenty? Fifty? She had long lost count. She

stared up at the ceiling and saw her childhood as clearly as a
scene revealed in a flash of lightning: the way she used to follow
the cracks in the ceiling, waiting for sleep, soothed by the soft
neighing of this ancient house.

And:

The next day they checked out the barns, and were aston-
ished to find a horse tethered to a fence post, a heap of bur-
nished hay piled up beside him. "Who's this?" Harriet asked,
and the horse seemed to respond, unhorselike, with an odd
creaking that came from the back of its throat.

Reversing the sounds in these two passages is quite effective. The
house takes on a personality of its own, and the horse becomes something more than a horse—a creature with something to say. Is the
horse ill? Lonesome? Hostile? That "odd creaking" could mean a lot
of things, and the readers are suddenly standing at attention.

One last thing: Don't worry about getting kicked out of the writers' union for using a thesaurus. A thesaurus is a wonderful (striking;
marvelous; fabulous; wondrous; etc.) resource for finding new ways
to describe sound (or anything else, for that matter). Suppose you
want to describe a bird's nest falling out of a tree during a windstorm,
and the only word you can think of for the sound of impact is
"thump." The word doesn't seem quite right; the nest is too delicate
to make a thump. In the thesaurus under "thump" you find the
following synonyms: beat; pulse; throb; flutter; hit; slap; poke. Not
quite. You look up the synonyms for the synonyms. Under "throb,"
for example, you find these possibilities: tick; flutter; tremble; tingle;
thrill; twitter. Nothing there, either, except that the word "twitter"
reminds you that the nest is full of twittering baby birds. Now you
want a word to describe two sounds at once: the falling nest and the
agitated birds. Look up "twitter": tremble; thrill; quaver; quiver. Nice
word, "quiver." You decide that maybe the thump is right after all,
as long as you add other nuances of sound to the description of the
falling nest:

John braced for the worst gust of the morning. He looked
up just as the air began to roil. High in the willow, a burgeoning
nest quivered briefly in the wind, then twittered to the ground
and landed with a thump at his feet.

"Twitter" as a verb for motion rather than sound ("the nest . . . twittered to the ground . . .") is apt, for it accurately describes the visual teetering motion of the nest while suggesting the sound of the birds. "Twittered" (rather than "plummeted" or "fell") suggests the lightness of the nest in the windy air, leaving the word "thump" as an entirely appropriate sound-word to describe its final drop to the ground.

Sound-words are best used sparingly. Most of the time a simple description of the source of the sound is enough: "She heard the cat outside, walking over the gravel." No sound-word needed—and each reader hears something different.

WRAP-UP

Descriptions can be problematic, some more than others. Whenever you run into trouble, remember the fundamentals: telling detail, simile and metaphor, engaging the senses. By applying these fundamentals to all descriptive situations, you can describe virtually anything in a way that readers can hear, feel, and see. Animals require the same range of color and shape that you would give to a description of people. Sensory details are as important to describing weather as they are to describing landscapes. Finding just the right word for a sound is not much different from finding just the right word for a character's hair. Describing an emotion by identifying the right gesture is not much different from describing a fence by identifying the shape of the pickets.

Good description is only partly a mystery. Mostly, it is the wise application of a few sensible rules. With a little patience and determination, you can find exactly the right words to describe a snow leopard or a snow job or a snowstorm. This search is what makes writing such a continual and satisfying surprise.

CHAPTER 9

TIPS AND TRICKS

A COMPENDIUM OF ADVICE THAT SUMMARIZES some of the concepts already discussed in the book, this chapter looks a little like a workbench: if you pick and sort long enough, you'll find exactly the tool you didn't realize you were looking for. Some of the tips are new—random offerings that did not fit logically into any particular chapter but were worth noting anyway.

I hope you will use this chapter to rummage around for ideas and inspiration when you're struggling with a scene or having trouble getting from one part of a story to another. Suggestions given out of context can sometimes strike the right chord in a way an entire chapter devoted to one problem cannot. So, when you're stuck, or daydreaming, or otherwise not writing, scan the following tips and tricks to get you back on your way.

Expand your field of vision. Experienced bird-watchers know that different species of warblers feed at different heights on a tree. They look to the top for Blackburnians, across the middle for Magnolias, and in the lower branches for Black-and-Whites. Experienced writers follow the same instinct when observing people or nature. Don't get so focused on the sky that you miss the ground. A person's kneecaps might be as defining as his nose. The squeak of a person's shoes could be as telling as the squeak of his voice. Look up, down, all around for the details that best capture the thing you are describing.

Go beyond red, white, and blue. Don't be afraid to liven up your descriptions by getting creative with color. Cerulean is not exactly blue, russet is not exactly red. Describe the color of things with familiar objects: a jacket can be the color of eggplant, hair can be the color of hay. Mustard-colored, storm-colored, cabbage-colored, money-colored—all these colors say something not only about the object being described, but about the observer, too.

Circle your adverbs. Too many adverbs is a sign that you aren't working hard enough to let language transfer a scene from your eyes to the readers'. When reviewing your work, watch for unnecessary, irrelevant, or extraneous adverbs (especially the ones that end in "ly"). If you describe a main character as one who behaves "lovingly" and works "tirelessly" only to come home to a family that treats her "terribly," which causes her to speak to them "bitterly"—you have a description problem. You are describing things in the abstract rather than in the particular. Instead of telling us that the heroine works tirelessly, describe the callouses on her hands or her slow and heavy walk. Examine your adverbs to make sure you aren't forcing them to do the hard work of observation for you. They can't.

And while you're at it, circle your adjectives. Good description is not defined by the number of adjectives per sentence. When in the editing phase of writing you might try literally counting adjectives in any given paragraph. Paradoxically, a string of adjectives (no matter how bright and punchy) can diminish the descriptive power of a moment. For example, a sentence like "He turned his slack, reddened face to the white-hot, midday sun" is made flabby and unnoticeable by too many adjectives. "He turned his face to the white-hot sun" is direct and more dramatic.

Turn a bland simile into a vivid adjective. Similes can sometimes seem like a writer's desperate attempt to depict a vivid world. Turning similes into adjectives can help you vary your descriptive style and still retain the comparisons that help readers see what you see. "He had a face like a cabbage" can be converted to "his cabbage-like face." "She moved like a duck" becomes "her ducklike walk." "James dropped from roof to balcony, quick as a cat" becomes "his feline leap." Similarly, a description like "When George laughed he seemed to roar like a lion" can be made more effective with adjectives: "George unleashed a leonine [or lionlike] roar of a laugh." Or, you could skip both simile and adjective and simplify the description this way: "George roared."

Don't mix metaphors. The mixed metaphor gets first prize for exposing beginning writers. Metaphor disasters abound in most writers' early (and mercifully unpublished) work, whether they care to admit it or not. To wit: "Without her, he was a bird shot from the sky, his very foundation crumbling under the rotting timbers of his widowhood." This sentence looks amateurish and overwritten because conflicting metaphors are crowding each other off the page. Go with the bird or the house, but don't include them both. Birds don't have foundations or rotting timbers, and houses don't get shot out of the sky. You might try something like "... he was a bird shot out of the sky, suddenly wingless, crying out in disbelief" or "... he was no more stable than the house across the road, his foundation crumbling under the rotting timbers of his widowhood." In any case, don't make metaphors too obvious, as both of these are.

Tone down your metaphors. In the above tip, the metaphors are so heavy-handed as to be amateurish even once they've been unmixed. If you want to compare the poor guy to a wingless bird, you might lay out the *suggestion* of a bird instead of coming at us full-tilt with "he *was* a bird. ..." For example, he could be sitting in his garden noticing that all the birds are showing up in pairs for the nesting season, or perhaps he could remember shooting birds when he was a child and *then* be reminded of their "crying out in disbelief." Metaphors that begin with "he *was* a lion" ("he was a lion of a man" is better) or "she *was* a cat" are usually too loaded at the outset to work. If you write, "She curled into the chair, catlike, and brushed the lint carefully off one sleeve, then the other," you give the character over to the metaphor of a cat without actually calling her a cat. Her deliberate movements ("first one sleeve, then the other") are reminiscent of the way cats groom themselves; the mere suggestion is enough to paint the picture.

Use the impersonal pronoun for animals. To avoid sentimentality, describe animals as "it" rather than "he" or "she." "The cat fetched its kittens one by one and carried them into the other closet" sounds less sentimental than "The cat carried her kittens . . ." The impersonal pronoun allows animals to remain animals. Leave the personal pronouns for the characters themselves to use. "She bit me twice," a first-person narrator might say of his dog, but a third-person narrative would read "The dog bit its master twice."

Jazz up your prose by engaging the senses. When a descriptive passage fails for no reason that you can easily discern, take a good look at your sensory details. Are they all visual? Add a sound or a scent to get the prose moving again.

Don't rely on brand names. If you present a character who wakes up on a Beautyrest mattress, eats a bowl of Cheerios cereal, laces up her Reebok sneakers, and grabs her Gucci briefcase before bicycling to work on her Bianchi mountain bike, you run the risk of creating an annoyed reader rather than a "real" character. Use brand names only when they serve to illuminate something about character or story. The Cheerios might be important if the character has been fighting with her kids over their crummy eating habits; the Reeboks might be important if the character spent a week deciding whether or not to take up jogging. It's hard to imagine any reason to include a Gucci briefcase in a description of anything except a briefcase store.

Don't use "telling" names. Who can forget Snidley Whiplash or Cruella DeVille, cartoon villains we loved to hate? Names like that work great in cartoons. Unfortunately, unless you're Charles Dickens, giving characters descriptive names only diminishes serious fiction. A track star named Bea Swift is going to seem like a cartoon character, no matter what your intentions. If you're writing humor or satire, then by all means name away—but for serious fiction, "telling" names won't do the job.

You can work with sounds when naming characters, however. A heartless surgeon might be made more vivid with a name like "Dr. Crutchfield" or "Dr. Hatch"—sounds that are reminiscent of ripping or tearing. The association isn't Snidley-Whiplash obvious, but does add just a dash of menace to the character. A kind old woman might be well served by a name like "Polly": the sound is round and soft.

The right name can make a character come into focus not only for your readers, but for you.

Don't use alien names. The above advice can be reversed: You shouldn't give your characters names that are too obviously meant to reveal their character, but neither should you give them names that are too alien to their character. For example, if you invent a wealthy, upper-crust English landowner with a name like Luther Johnson, you'd better be prepared to explain how he came by that name (it could be the heart of the story). On the other hand, if you write about an American sharecropper named Neville Windsor, a similar explanation is in order. (I, for one, would love to hear it.)

Don't pile on the details. Too many details in a passage of prose can obscure its meaning. For example, the story of a social worker visiting the house of a notoriously recalcitrant family could begin this way:

> The mud in the grassless yard was about two inches thick, at first spongy and yielding under her feet. She moved through the litter-strewn pathway to the house, through the spare parts of long-forgotten cars, sun-bleached Popsicle wrappers, coils of rope, tatters of ink-smeared junk mail, various and colorful plastic parts from several generations of children's toys, junked wood that had once been part of several decent but inexpensive discount-store furniture, clay pots with jagged cracks, and an inexplicable assortment of kites in various stages of decay. Alice picked her way through the obstacle course, aware of the low and glowering sky above her that carried the tang of sulphur from the mill downriver. She shifted her briefcase from one arm to the other, aware of its weight and heft and how it must make her look—like a bureaucrat from the state come to torture some unsuspecting family. She looked up to find the lady of the house, a massive woman in a calico apron, staring like an owl from behind the screen door. Alice smiled and waved as the mud began to pull at her shoes, making each step forward like a leap through time and space.

This is a lot of detail, and in the right story it could work just fine. Know, however, that you always have the option of weeding out details so the readers can see the forest for the trees. You don't have to set up a scene by describing everything from the weather to the buttons on the character's blouse. Keep in mind the central image you yourself can see when entering your character's world:

> Alice picked her way through the pulling mud, her eye on the massive woman behind the screen door. Each step was harder than the first—besides the mud she had to watch for discarded car parts and broken toys—and she began to believe she was moving in great, agonizing leaps through time and space.

More detail is not always better. Every once in a while you have to remember to let your prose breathe!

Use adjectives in surprising ways. Try to write description that contains verbal surprises. An adjective like "sweet" does not always have to describe sugar, or a kitten, or a baby. How about a sweet tractor, or a sweet hurricane? Flex those adjectives! In the right story, seemingly unrelated adjective-noun combinations—frightful goodness, ferocious necklace, barnlike body—can strike exactly the descriptive note you want.

Don't use unusual adjectives twice. Common adjectives like "small," "large," "brown," or "wet" can be repeated in a story, sometimes three or four times, without drawing attention to themselves. Less common adjectives, however—"lissome," "electrifying," "fractious," "sinister"—should be used only once per story. A good adjective repeated becomes a bad word choice.

Check for descriptive consistency. If Dorothy has blue eyes on page two, then she'd better have blue eyes on page nine. You'd be surprised how often inconsistencies crop up. If you write only on weekends, or are rewriting a story you began five years ago, you are especially prone to having descriptive inconsistencies.

Don't mix up point of view. Any description of a character or place or event takes on a particular perspective. That perspective may be your own, or a first-person narrator's, or a third-person narrator's—whatever point of view you choose, stay consistent. The third-person narrator might see the clear blue sky as ominous; the main character might see the same sky as a sign of good luck; the "camera eye" would objectively record the sky as blue. Don't call the sky ominous on page one and lucky on page five unless you've clearly and deliberately shifted point of view. Decide who's calling the descriptive shots right at the beginning.

Don't enslave yourself to "showing." "Show, don't tell" is a guideline, not a rule. Sometimes telling is more effective than showing. A brief statement—"Helen was a cheat. It was that simple"— may be far more effective than a two-page scene showing Helen at work as a cheat. Telling can be just as thrilling as showing as long as the prose is interesting and engaging.

Elevate the mundane with some lyricism. When describing things that are inherently dull—a pig farm, for example—inject some fresh imagery and lyrical phraseology into the description. The pigs might resemble failed dictators, say; the hoof-marked mud might be hardened in spots and reminiscent of an elegant, pressed-tin ceiling; the setting sun might cast ribbons of color over the sagging fences. Beauty and ugliness exist in everything we see if we're willing to look hard enough.

Avoid sentimentality and melodrama. Sentimentality runs rampant when we write in abstractions: "She was wracked with grief." "His happiness knew no bounds." Avoid melodrama by sticking to accessible, concrete images: "She covered her face with her hands." "He ran down the green slope of lawn, his long hair spraying out like a fireworks." Describe the things we can see or hear; we can't see or hear "wracked" any more than we can see or hear "no bounds." We can, however, see a woman's hands on her face or a man's hair spraying out as he runs.

Avoid "realistic" details that alienate the readers. Say you're writing a story about an ornithologist. You don't know much about birds yourself, so you flee to the library to research the science of birds. That's fine. Drink it in. Learn all you can until your ornithologist's motivations and passions are as familiar as your own. When you finally sit down to write the story, though, don't treat your readers to the fruits of your labors. *You* should know the difference between *altricial* and *precocial*, but your readers don't necessarily have to. People love to learn new things through fiction, but only if the story itself remains center stage. Introduce unfamiliar words or facts as part of the story's natural unfolding. Resist the temptation to show off; your hard work should be invisible by the time it gets to the page. The only purpose of all your bird research is to make your character, the ornithologist, believable to the readers. Jargon words like *passerine* and *syrinx* will alienate your readers, while the lay terms—*perching bird* and *voicebox*—will allow them into the fascinating world of birds. The paradox of fiercely researched stories is that the more technical terms you throw in, the more the readers figure you don't really know what you're talking about. It looks like overcompensation. If you're such an expert on the migratory pattern of scissor-tailed flycatchers, then why can't you explain it in plain English? If you *must* use jargon (perhaps that's the way the character talks), then take care to explain in some other way what the words mean:

> "Here's where the damage is," Dr. Hendrix said. He examined the cardinal's orange beak, working it open and closed with his fingers. "Do you see how the upper and lower mandibles aren't closing properly?"

Certain unfamiliar words can be worked into context, of course—you don't want to insult your readers by going too far in the direction of simplicity. Just remember that you're writing a story, not a textbook, and that the character himself should be more interesting than the work he does.

Don't abuse your thesaurus. Thesauruses are life-savers, but they can't turn bad prose into good. If you find yourself running to the thesaurus every five minutes then you aren't working hard enough. If you want just the right word to describe your mother's garden, don't expect the thesaurus to provide it. You're better off sitting in your mother's garden for half an hour and taking in the experience of what you would like to describe.

Use description to place dialogue in context. Conversations don't take place in a vacuum. People talk while eating, cleaning house, shoveling snow, appraising jewelry, committing murder. A descriptive tag as simple as " . . . she said, giving the cement mixer another turn" can remind your readers that the characters are not talking heads and that a story is in progress.

Above all, enjoy yourself! We all have something to say. We all have joys and sorrows and magical moments in our past that shape our unique view of the human condition. Sharing our view through the written word should be the easiest thing in the world. It isn't, though; sometimes it's the hardest thing in the world. Writing is tough work. It requires time, and concentration, and self-confidence, and extraordinary patience. This is true whether you're writing your first story or your hundredth. Because the writing process requires so much from us, we often get frustrated or discouraged or just plain furious about the whole thing. When this happens, remind yourself that writing is supposed to be fun. Don't take yourself so seriously. If the story you're writing now never sees publication, so what? I can look back on dozens of my own unpublished stories and see them as the steps that led to the published ones. Nothing you write is ever wasted! Like the basketball player who spends every morning shooting nothing but free throws, you have to practice to get better. On those days when you feel like a tongue-tied hack, remind yourself why you write. Remind yourself of the joy your own words can bring you. Remind yourself how good it feels to finish a first draft. Remind yourself how satisfying it is to finally send a story out with hope and a prayer. It's the process, not the product, that brings the most satisfaction. Not all of us will see the product—a published story—but the process is ours for the taking. No entry fee, no prerequisites—just a pencil and an idea.

INDEX

Other Books in the Elements of Fiction Writing Series

Setting—Don't ignore setting as a key to powerful, moving fiction. Bickham, author of over 80 published novels, demonstrates how to use sensual detail and vivid language to paint the perfect setting for your story.
ISBN-13: 978-0-89879-948-4, paperback, 176 pages, #10646
ISBN-10: 0-89879-948-1, paperback, 176 pages, #10646

Scene & Structure—Whatever the form or length of your story, it needs scene-by-scene flow, logic and readability. Bickham uses dozens of examples from his bestselling novels to help you build a sturdy framework for your novel.
ISBN-13: 978-0-89879-906-4, paperback, 168 pages, #10606
ISBN-10: 0-89879-906-6, paperback, 168 pages, #10606

Beginnings, Middles & Ends—Award-winning author, Kress, uses concrete instruction and dozens of exercises to show you how to get stories off to a roaring start, keep them tight throughout and end them with a wallop!
ISBN-13: 978-0-89879-905-7, paperback, 149 pages, #10605
ISBN-10: 0-89879-905-8, paperback, 149 pages, #10605

Characters & Viewpoint—Discover how to make your work come alive with vivid, credible, true-to-life characters. Card shows you how to choose the best vantage point for your reader to see the events of your short story or novel unfold.
ISBN-13: 978-0-89879-927-9, paperback, 182 pages, #10620
ISBN-10: 0-89879-927-9, paperback, 182 pages, #10620

Plot—Don't let your novel or short story sag in the middle or fizzle out at the end. Dibell shares dozens of secrets and techniques for building and sustaining gripping, memorable plots.
ISBN-13: 978-0-89879-946-0, paperback, 176 pages, #10644
ISBN-10: 0-89879-946-5, paperback, 176 pages, #10644

These and other fine Writer's Digest titles are available from your local bookstore or online supplier.